Wildflowers
of the
Berkshires

Where and When They Bloom
Vol. 2

Phyllis Pryzby

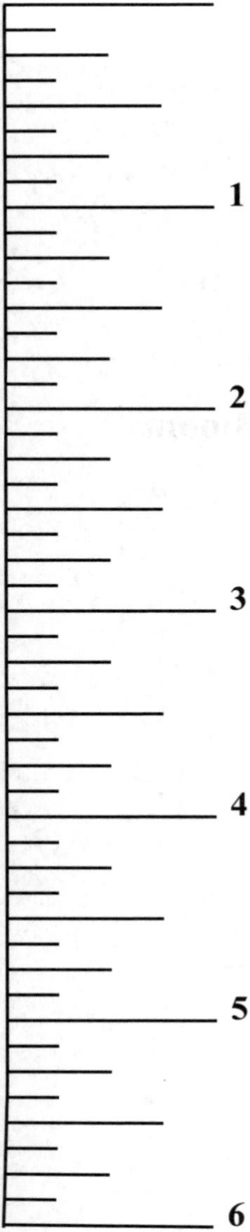
1
2
3
4
5
6

Wildflowers of the Berkshires

Where and When They Bloom

Vol. 2

by Phyllis Pryzby

Photographs by the Author

ISBN 0-9700509-2-5

Due to changes in conditions, use of
the information in this book is at the
sole risk of the user.

Published by Phyllis Pryzby

Printed in the United States of America by
The Studley Press
Dalton, Massachusetts

*To my husband, John, who spent
many hours helping me to make
this book a reality.*

Contents

INTRODUCTION

From The Author

There are wonderful wildflowers along the many trails and paths in Berkshire County. I experience a certain excitement when I see a new, beautiful flower and also experience pleasure when seeing one that I have seen before. I hope this book will lead my readers to similar enjoyment.

Five additional wildflower locations I have documented are found in *Wildflowers of the Berkshires: Where and When They Bloom, Volume 1.*

Ways To Use This Book

To determine when a certain wildflower blooms.

To find out which flowers bloom at the locations mentioned in this book.

To learn the names of wildflowers.

To determine which flowers bloom in the woods and which bloom in fields.

Method of Gathering Information

I gathered the information for this book by walking along specific trails and paths for several years at Benedict Pond, Pleasant Valley and Canoe Meadows Wildflower Sanctuaries, the trails across from Hancock Shaker Village, and by the Arrowhead wildflower garden.   As I walked, I listed the flowers I saw blooming. Each area was checked twice a month, once during the first two weeks and once during the last two weeks.

Early and Late Seasons

I noticed that some flowers bloomed earlier some years and later in others, especially in spring. Late seasons seemed to occur as a result of cold spring weather or a late snowfall. In order to document these differences, I included lists for both early and late seasons.

Differences in Flowers Observed Each Year

I found that some flowers bloomed in one year, but not in others, so I included information from all the years.

From my observations and reading articles on flowers, I have concluded that differences in flowers observed in various years may be accounted for as follows:

1) Some flowers bloomed, but I did not see them.

2) Some flowers bloomed before or after I took my walks.

3) Some flowers don't bloom every year. An example is the Pink Lady's Slipper [Moccasin Flower], which is a perennial (having a life cycle of more than two years). According to the New England Wildflower Society, this plant, if left undisturbed, may live for 100 years but only bloom some years, more likely when a tree falls down and the canopy opens up.

4) Some flowers bloom only part of the day. Yellow Goatsbeard blooms only in the morning and Chicory and Sweet-scented Water Lily bloom in the morning and early afternoon.

5) Seeds produced by annuals (plants that live for one year) or biennials (plants that live for two years, blooming only in the second) have reseeded themselves elsewhere.

6) Biennials were in their first year of growth and did not bloom.

7) Climatic conditions were different in one year than the other. This aided the growth of some plants and discouraged or prevented the growth of others.

8) Some plants or flowers might have been picked or mowed, causing a plant to bloom late or not at all.

Preservation of Flower Species

I hope my readers will resist the urge to pick the flowers they see, especially the unusual ones, since picking flowers makes it impossible for plants to produce seeds for reproduction.

Mowing an area before flowering plants have been able to produce their seeds also has a negative effect. Annuals (plants that live only one year) and biennials (plants that live two years) are especially vulnerable to extinction from an area since they depend exclusively on seed production for propagation.

Attempts to transplant wildflowers may kill many of them, either because conditions in the new area are not conducive to their growth or because they are extremely difficult to transplant. Taking wildflowers from their natural habitats will also make it impossible for other hikers to enjoy them. Therefore, I am hoping my readers will enjoy the flowers they see, but leave them where they are growing.

If any of my readers are interested in growing wildflowers in their own garden, the New England Wildflower Society sells both wildflower seeds and plants as well as directions on how to grow them.

Their address is:

New England Wild Flower Society, Inc.
Garden in the Woods
180 Hemenway Road
Framingham, MA 01701-2699

Their website is: www.newfs.org

Flower Listing

I used *Newcomb's Wildflower Guide* by Lawrence Newcomb as my primary source for wildflower names. They are listed by common names. In cases where there was more than one common name, they are listed in the order given in Newcomb's book with the second and/or third name in brackets. For example: Pink Azalea [Pinxter Flower] means Pink Azalea is the first name and Pinxter Flower is the second name given in Newcomb's book. Cow [Tufted] Vetch means Newcomb's book has it listed as Cow or Tufted Vetch. This means it can be called Cow Vetch or Tufted Vetch. False

[White] Hellibore [Indian Poke] means this plant can be called False Hellibore, White Hellibore, or Indian Poke.

For those with a knowledge of scientific names, I have included two indices - one of scientific names with their common name equivalents and another of common names with their scientific name equivalents.

The flowers listed in this book are only those I personally saw blooming. The lists may not be totally comprehensive, but will be accurate to what I saw on my walks. Since there is a fine line between garden flowers and wildflowers, I included the garden perennials and shrubs that I observed on my walks as well as wildflowers. To give a picture of what a visitor might expect, I often commented on the flowers I saw in a certain area. These comments are surrounded by parentheses. Examples are (many), (few), (beginning to bloom), etc.

I decided not to list very common flowers that bloom almost everywhere, green flowers, and some of the very small flowers. Examples of common flowers would be Dandelions, Yellow Wood Sorrel, Garlic Mustard, and Selfheal [Heal-all]. Clovers are not mentioned except White Sweet Clover.

To simplify the lists, I did not mention the species of some genera. Goldenrods, for instance, have been lumped together with the exception of Zigzag [Broad-leaved] Goldenrod, Blue-stemmed [Wreath] Goldenrod and Silverrod. Similarly, Violets have been differentiated only by color of flower except Dame's Violet. The species of Blue-eyed Grass, Buttercups, some Chokeberries, and Raspberries (other than Purple-flowering and Black Raspberry) were also not mentioned.

Most flowers that are Endangered, Threatened or of Special Concern have not been mentioned for their protection.

Photographs

I brought my camera on most walks and took pictures of the flowers I observed. Many of these pictures are included in this book to aid in identification. They are listed in the index in bold type.

Size and Arrangement of Flower Pictures

The size of the flowers of each species varies somewhat, but also stays within certain parameters. The pictures in this book indicate the approximate size of each flower by the size of the picture and a size indicator written at the right of the flower name. The size indicators tell how large the picture is compared with the flower. One example would be (x 1/2) which would mean that the picture is half as large as the flower. Another would be (x 2/5) meaning that that the flower picture is 2/5ths as large as the flower.

The pictures in this book are organized by the shapes of the flowers and arrangement of the leaves.

Explanation of Terms Used to Describe Shapes of Flowers

Regular flowers: Flowers that have petals or petal-like parts that are similar to each other in shape, size, and color and are arranged around the center like spokes of a wheel. If the petals are united, as in bell-shaped flowers, they are considered regular if the lobes (outer rounded parts) are similar in shape, size, and color.

Some flowers with regular parts have petals that are somewhat divided and can appear to have more petals than they do. Examples would be shapes like:

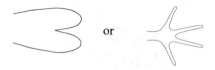

Therefore, in determining the number of petals, one must observe them from their point of origin. A magnifying glass often helps to do this.

Irregular flowers: Flowers that have petals that are <u>not</u> similar in shape, size, and color and are <u>not</u> symmetrical.

Indistinguishable flowers: Flowers that have no noticeable petal-like parts or have parts so small that their numbers or arrangement is difficult to discern. Be aware, however, that some flowers may have parts that are recognizable if seen under a magnifying glass, so they may be listed by the shape and number of petals even though appearing indistinguishable to the naked eye.

Explanation of Terms Used to Describe the Arrangement of Leaves

Note: When trying to determine the arrangement of leaves on the main stem, observe an area where the leaves are widely spaced so their arrangement is distinct.

Basal leaves only: Leaves growing only from the base of the plant.

Stem leaves: Leaves growing on the main stem of the plant.

Opposite leaves: Leaves growing directly across from each other on the main stem.

Example:

<u>Caution:</u> Some plants have what appear to be secondary stems branching from the main stem with leaves on each branch. The apparent leaves are opposite each other on this secondary stem. This stem may even divide again into two opposite stems. This arrangement can be misinterpreted as being opposite leaves. However, if their connection to the <u>main</u> stem is alternate, not opposite, they are considered to be <u>divided leaves</u> with several leaflets arranged <u>alternately</u> on the <u>main</u> stem.

Four examples of two divided [segmented] leaves arranged alternately on the main stem:

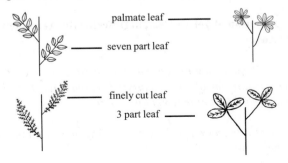

palmate leaf ⎯⎯⎯

⎯⎯ seven part leaf

finely cut leaf

3 part leaf ⎯⎯⎯

Whorled leaves: Leaves growing in circles of three or more around the main stem in one or more places on the stem.

Alternate leaves: Leaves arranged singly (not opposite) on the main stem. Leaves vary in shape and can be either simple or divided.

two divided leaves arranged
alternately on the stem

Examples:

General Shapes of Leaves

There is a wide variety of shapes in leaves. Some have straight edges, some are toothed, some are lobed, and some are divided with several leaflets (see the four examples on page xviii). However, I am including only information about shapes of leaves that is necessary for use in this book.

Heart-shaped leaves: Leaves in the shape of a valentine heart.

Example:

Lance-shaped leaves: Leaves that are wider at one end and narrow to a point at the other end, usually three or more times longer than wide.

Examples of lance-shaped leaves mentioned in the picture section:

Narrowly lance-shaped

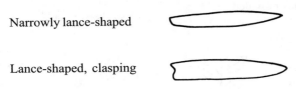

Lance-shaped, clasping

Clasping leaves (leaves that clasp stem): Leaves that begin directly at the stem and surround the stem part way.

Example:

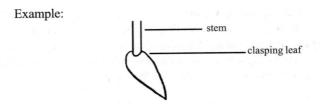

stem

clasping leaf

Explanation of Unusually-shaped Stem

Winged stem: The stem that joins the leaf to the main stem is wider than usual. Lowrie's Aster is identified by a winged stem.

Example:

winged stem _____

Books Used as Sources of Information

I used *Newcomb's Wildflower Guide* as my primary source for the names of the flowers. Occasionally, I also used *Wildflowers* by Peterson, *Field Guide to North American Wildflowers* by the Audubon Society, and *Encyclopedia of Flowers,* Mary Moody, general editor. Wildflower names in this book are from *Newcomb's Wildflower Guide.*

Information on possible areas to explore in the Berkshires came from René Laubach's *Guide to Natural Places,* Charles W. G. Smith's *Nature Walks in the Berkshire Hills,* and Joseph G. Strauch, Jr.'s *Wildflowers of the Berkshire and Taconic Hills..*

Acknowledgements

I received help from many people whom I would like to thank. I owe the most to my husband, John, who did the computer work for the index, pictures, covers, and part of the introduction. He also edited the introduction, taught me how to operate the computer, and gave me suggestions and encouragement.

I also received encouragement, helpful suggestions, and information from many other people. These include René Laubach and Laura Tate Beltran of the Massachusetts Audubon Society, Fred Blair from Beartown State Forest, Don Reid of the Trustees of Reservations, and Susan Eisley and Janet Cook from the Berkshire County Historical Society.

I also received information from the staff of the Department of Environmental Management, Division of Forests and Parks, the staff of Hancock Shaker Village, and

Pamela Weatherby from Williamstown. I would also like to thank Marion Thompson and Joan Biros for their encouragement and helpful suggestions.

I would like to express my appreciation to the Massachusetts Department of Environmental Management, Division of Forests and Parks, the Massachusetts Audubon Society, the Berkshire County Historical Society, and Hancock Shaker Village for allowing me to use their propery for my research.

DRIVING, FACILITIES, AND TRAIL INFORMATION

Benedict Pond

Driving Directions-

From Massachusetts Turnpike Exit 2: From the exit turn left onto Route 20 East and then take an immediate right onto Route 102 West. Continue on Route 102 West into Stockbridge where it joins Route 7 South. Follow Routes 7 and 102, then stay on Route 7 South when they separate just past the center of town. Continue on Route 7 South and look for Monument Mountain Regional School on your left. Immediately after the school, turn left onto Monument Valley Road. Go 2 miles to Stony Brook Road. Bear left onto Stony Brook Road and continue 3 miles to Benedict Pond Road. Turn left onto Benedict Pond Road and go 0.3 miles to a large parking lot or 0.4 miles to a small parking lot near the swimming area.

What to expect-

Benedict Pond is part of Beartown State Forest and is owned by the Massachusetts Department of Environmental Management Division of Forests and Parks. Beartown State Forest is open all year. The trails are open from dawn to dusk. There is a $5.00 parking charge from Memorial Day weekend to Labor Day weekend.

Rest rooms with flush toilets are located near the swimming area and are open when the weather is warm. There are also compost toilets which are open all year. They can be found by driving past the small parking lot, down the hill, and up the next hill.

According to Massachusetts State Park rules, nobody should damage, take, or remove anything from Massachusetts State Forests and Parks. Exceptions are made by a specific permit from the director of the Massachusetts Department of Forests and Parks. Pets are allowed, but they must be on a leash in camping areas or beaches. Check with the park supervisor whether a leash is required in other areas.

Trail Information-

<u>Pond Loop Trail:</u> The trail is approximately 1.5 miles and can be hiked in about 53 minutes at a moderate pace without stopping. The trail has a few ups and downs, but is basically level.

A pamphlet, provided by Beartown State Forest with a map and a self-guided walking tour of the Pond Loop Trail, is at the right hand corner of the large parking lot. The self-guided walking tour begins here. However, my wildflower walk begins to the left of the swimming area.

Begin walking from the left of the swimming area along the pond toward a small bridge. Cross the bridge and continue to a sign 'Pond Loop Trail'. Go left at the sign and follow the trail around the lake. (Last time I looked the sign was blank on the side I was coming from and had the words on the other side.)

The trail is marked primarily by *blue* or *white* paint on trees and a few signs. Be sure to watch for the next markers, especially at the beginning of the trail because there are connecting trails that lead to camp sites and *another* trail that is marked with *red* paint. The Pond Loop Trail goes all the way around the pond. It has a great variety of flowers, especially near the edge of the pond.

Pleasant Valley Wildlife Sanctuary

Driving Directions-

<u>From Massachusetts Turnpike Exit 2</u>: Turn right and follow Route 20 West for 6.7 miles. Then turn left onto West Dugway Road in Lenox. Go 0.8 miles. Bear left at a fork in the road and continue on West Mountain Road 0.8 miles to Pleasant Valley. Parking is just off the road.

What to expect-

Pleasant Valley Wildlife Sanctuary (Pleasant Valley) is owned by the Massachusetts Audubon Society. The trails are open from sunrise to dusk seven days a week from late June through Columbus Day. They are open from sunrise to dusk Tuesday through Sunday for the rest of the year. Dogs are not allowed. No hunting, firearms, fishing, trapping, or collecting of living or dead material is allowed.

Entrance is free to Massachusetts Audubon Society members and Lenox residents. The entrance fee for non-member adults is $5.00 from July through Columbus Day and $4.00 throughout the rest of the year. The fee for non-member seniors age 65 and above and non-member children is consistent throughout the year. Seniors are $3.00 and children $3.00. They keep track of visitors, so be sure to stop at the office window near the entrance and register. There are rest rooms past the entrance to the left.

Trail Information-

A trail map and other information is provided at the office window. The trails are well marked by signs and paint markers. Blue markers indicate trails leading away from the office and yellow markers indicate trails leading toward the office.

<u>Pike's Pond Trail</u>: This trail is approximately 0.5 miles and can be hiked in about 15 minutes if you hike at a moderate pace without stopping.

After checking in at the office, go down the steps and follow the path. Turn right and pass the office building on the right and the barn on the left. (The building on the left has attached rest rooms down the stairs.) The hummingbird/ butterfly garden is to your right just behind the office. Continue downhill to the Pike's Pond Trail sign. Turn left at the sign. Follow the path around the pond to the end of the loop. This trail traverses some fields, but is mostly bordered by the pond and woods. It is quite level except for one set of steps.

<u>Honeysuckle Lane:</u> This trail is 0.03 miles and can be hiked in about 1 minute if you hike at a moderate pace without stopping.

This very short trail connects the two ends of the Pike's Pond Trail and roughly parallels the Bluebird Trail.. To find this trail from the office, go straight from the steps rather than turning right. Continue straight to the sign Honeysuckle Lane.

Loop beginning at Bluebird Trail: The loop is about 0.7 miles long and can be hiked in approximately 32 minutes at a moderate pace without stopping.

After checking in at the office, go down the steps and follow the path. Turn right and pass the office building on the right and the barn on the left. (The barn on the left has attached rest rooms down the stairs.) The hummingbird/butterfly garden is to your right just after the office. Continue down the hill and past the sign for the Pike's Pond trail. Continue straight at the Bluebird Trail/Alexander Trail sign and follow this trail down through the field and into the woods.

Turn right at Yokun Trail (just before the bridge over Yokun Brook). Follow this trail to the Old Wood Road sign. Turn left at this sign, cross the bridge, and follow the path back into the woods until you come to the Beaver Lodge Trail. Turn left onto this trail and follow it back to the Bluebird Trail. Go left and then left again at trail intersections, then cross two brooks and follow the yellow markers straight back to the entrance path. Continue up the hill to the parking lot.

This trail starts in a field, but most of it goes through woods. Some portions are bordered by what appears to be a pond, but is actually Yokun Brook dammed up by beavers. The trail is quite level after the meadow descends to the wooded area.

Arrowhead

Driving Directions-

From Massachusetts Turnpike Exit 2: Turn right and follow Route 20 West for 8.2 miles. Turn right onto Holmes Road in Lenox. Go 1.5 miles and look for the Arrowhead sign on the left. Turn left by the sign and look for the parking lot in back of the house.

What to expect-

Arrowhead was Herman Melville's home for 13 years. It is now owned by the Berkshire County Historical Society and tours are given from Memorial Day weekend through October 31. The Visitor Center opens at 9:30. Tours are given 10:00 AM to 5:00 PM and start on the hour.

A very nice wildflower garden has been established by the Berkshire Garden Club. Visitors are not allowed to collect anything from the garden or the grounds of Arrowhead. The wildflower area and the rest of the grounds are open year round from sunrise to sunset. Dogs are allowed on the grounds as long as they are on a leash and the owners pick up after them. There is a fee for a tour of the house, but not for looking at the garden. A rest room in the barn is available during the hours when the house is open.

Trail Information-

Area with Wildflowers: Almost no walking. The Wildflower Garden is to the left of the exit road. I documented the flowers blooming in the garden as well as the ones blooming to the left of it.

Canoe Meadows Wildlife Sanctuary

Driving Directions-

From Massachusetts Turnpike Exit 2: Turn right and follow Route 20 West for 8.2 miles. Turn right at Holmes Road in Lenox. Go 2.8 miles. Look for the Canoe Meadows Wildlife Sanctuary sign on the right and turn right into the parking lot.

What to expect-

Canoe Meadows Wildlife Sanctuary (Canoe Meadows) is owned by the Massachusetts Audubon Society. Since this is a wildlife sanctuary, no collecting of plants, animals, rocks, or other natural objects is allowed. The trails and parking lot are open Tuesday through Sunday all year from 7 AM to dusk. No pets, hunting or trapping are allowed. There is no fee for Pittsfield residents and Massachusetts Audubon Society members. The fee for other adults is $3.00 and for children is $2.00. The fee should be left in the money pipe at the entrance. There are pit toilets in two places - near the entrance and about halfway down the road.

Trail Information-

Sacred Way Trail: This trail is 1.0 miles long and can be hiked in about 30 minutes at a moderate pace without stopping. It goes through meadows, woods, brush, and swampy areas and is quite level.

After a short walk down the road just past the parking lot, turn right at the sign for the Sacred Way Trail. Do not take the next left turn, but bear right and continue on the trail which soon goes over a footbridge. After crossing the bridge, turn right and continue on the main path around the Sacred Way Trail loop. To take the full loop, do not turn left at the Cross Over Trail. Continue on the main trail for quite a distance. When coming to the second Cross Over Trail sign (on the left side), bear right and go over several wooden boardwalks traversing swampy areas. Continue on the trail, and at a fork in the path bear right and cross the footbridge. Follow the path, bearing left twice, to the parking lot.

<u>Alternative Shorter Route beginning at the Sacred Way Trail and taking the Cross Over Trail:</u> This trail is about 0.3 miles and takes about 15 minutes if you hike at a moderate pace without stopping. It goes through meadows, woods, brush, and swampy areas and is quite level.

After a short walk down the road just past the parking lot, turn right at the sign for the Sacred Way Trail. Do not take the next left turn, but bear right and continue on the trail which soon goes over a footbridge. After crossing the bridge, turn right and continue on the path. Look on the left for a sign for the Cross Over Trail. Turn left at that sign. Taking the Cross Over Trail makes the walk shorter. There are many lovely flowers in the spring which are missed by taking the Cross Over Trail, so the long route is worth taking at that time. However, during the summer there are very few flowers and many mosquitoes on the long route, so the short route would be more enjoyable. After entering the Cross Over Trail, go for a short distance and then take a left. The trail goes over wooden boardwalks traversing swampy areas. Continue on the trail, and at a fork in the path bear right and cross the footbridge. Follow the path, bearing left twice, to the parking lot.

Service Road and Wolf Pine Trail: This trail is approximately 1.3 miles long and can be hiked in about 40 minutes at a moderate pace without stopping. The total trail goes through meadows, woods, brush, a causeway to a pond and swampy areas and is quite level. The Wolf Pine Trail is almost all woods.

Walk down the road from the parking lot without taking any turns and go all the way to the bridge. From the bridge you should see a man-made dam and hear running water. Turn around and go back toward the parking lot. Take the second right onto the Wolf Pine Trail. There may or may not be a sign as you are going into what may be considered an exit. Stay on this trail until it comes back to the road. Go right and follow the road back to the parking lot.

Trails across from the Hancock Shaker Village

Driving Directions-

From the junction of Routes 7 and 20 in Pittsfield (corner of South Street and West Housatonic Street), follow Route 20 West (West Housatonic Street) for 4.2 miles to the Hancock Shaker Village. Turn left into the Shaker Village parking lot. Go to the Visitor Center and tell them you would like to hike on their property across the street. They will give you a hiker's sticker, offer you a map of the trails, and give you directions to the trails.

What to expect-

Hancock Shaker Village is a restored original Shaker community. They own the trails across the highway from the main village area. There is a fee to tour the village, but no fee to walk the trails. The village is open all year. They are open from 9:30 AM to 5 PM from Memorial Day to the third week of October. The rest of the year they are open 10 AM to 3 PM. They prefer that hikers walk their trails when the village is open. To find the rest rooms, take the first door on the right on the way to the Visitor's Center. Dogs are allowed on the trails, but not in the historic part of the village. Since this is both a historical and natural area, plants, geological items, and archaeological remnants should not be collected.

Trail Information-

Round trip hiking distance to the 'Marble Quarry' sign and back to the highway is approximately 1.1 miles. Hiking time is about 38 minutes if hiked at a moderate pace without stopping.

After receiving a hiker's sticker at the Visitor Center, walk through the Village toward the cross walk as directed and cross the highway. Hike down the dirt road from the cross walk and through the field. Upon arriving at another road, turn right and enter a wooded area. Continue down this road past the foot bridge on the right and go uphill. When reaching a fork in the road, take the left fork and continue up another hill until you reach a sign for 'Marble Quarry'. Turn around and go back down the road, not turning into the meadow, but continuing toward the highway. I usually took the path to the left which went partway around the Shaker reservoir before continuing to the highway.

The trails are level except for the hills mentioned in the directions.

FIRST TWO WEEKS IN APRIL

Benedict Pond
See Trail Information for directions.

<u>Pond Loop Trail to left of swimming area</u>   *Early Season:*
Trailing Arbutus [Mayflower] (a few just beginning to bloom)

Late Season: No flowers were observed.

Pleasant Valley

<u>By office</u>*:*   *Early Season*: Siberian Scilla [Spring Squill]

Late Season: No flowers were observed.

<u>Path to Pike's Pond Trail</u>
See Trail Information for directions.

Early Season: Virginia Bluebells [Virginia Cowslip]

<u>Pike's Pond Trail</u>   *Early Season*:   Skunk Cabbage, Virginia Bluebells [Virginia Cowslip]

Late Season: Skunk Cabbage

<u>Honeysuckle Lane</u>   *See Trail Information for directions.*

Early and Late Seasons: No flowers were observed.

<u>Yokun Trail</u>   *See Trail Information for directions.*

Early and Late Seasons: Skunk Cabbage

Arrowhead
See Trail Information for directions to wildflower garden.

<u>Wildflower Garden</u>   *Early Season*: Siberian Scilla [Spring Squill]

Late Season: No flowers were observed.

<u>End of Driveway</u>   *Early Season*: Coltsfoot

Canoe Meadows

<u>Sacred Way Trail</u>   *See Trail Information for directions.*

Early and Late Seasons: No flowers were observed.

<u>Road</u>:   *See Trail Information for directions.*

Early Season: Siberian Scilla [Spring Squill], Bloodroot (beginning to bloom), Skunk Cabbage, Snowdrop [Early Snowdrop]

Late Season: Skunk Cabbage, Snowdrop [Early Snowdrop] (beginning to bloom)

<u>Wolf Pine Trail</u>   *Early Season*: Siberian Scilla [Spring Squill], Bloodroot, Skunk Cabbage, Snowdrop [Early Snowdrop]

Late Season: Skunk Cabbage, Snowdrop [Early Snowdrop] (beginning to bloom)

Trails across from Hancock Shaker Village
See Trail Information for directions.

<u>Road through field</u>   *Early and Late Seasons:* No flowers were observed.

<u>Road to right through woods</u>   *Early Season*: Bloodroot (beginning to bloom), Skunk Cabbage, Sharp-lobed Hepatica (white- few), Carolina Spring Beauty (few)

Late Season: Skunk Cabbage

<u>Road past field toward highway</u>   *Early Season*: Coltsfoot

Late Season: No flowers were observed.

LAST TWO WEEKS IN APRIL

Benedict Pond
See Trail Information for directions.

<u>Pond Loop Trail to left of swimming area</u>   *Early Season:*
Trailing Arbutus [Mayflower], Hobblebush

Late Season: Trailing Arbutus [Mayflower] (beginning to bloom)

Pleasant Valley

<u>Path to Pike's Pond Trail</u>
See Trail Information for directions.

Early and Late Seasons: Virginia Bluebells [Virginia Cowslip]

<u>Pike's Pond Trail</u> *Early Season*: Shadbush, Trailing Arbutus [Mayflower], Wake-robin [Birthroot, Purple or Red Trillium] (beginning to bloom), Skunk Cabbage, Marsh Marigold [Cowslip] (beginning to bloom), Siberian Scilla [Spring Squill], Virginia Bluebells [Virginia Cowslip], February Daphne

<u>Bluebird Trail</u> *See Trail Information for directions.*

Early Season: No flowers were observed.

<u>Yokun Trail to right</u>   *Early Season*: Bloodroot (very few), Skunk Cabbage, Wake-robin [Birthroot, Purple or Red Trillium] (few - beginning to bloom), Common Shadbush, Smooth Shadbush, Violet (purple), Bluets [Quaker Ladies, Innocence]

<u>Old Wood Road to left</u>   *Early Season*: Bluets [Quaker Ladies, Innocence]

<u>Beaver Lodge Trail to left</u>   *Early Season*: Some flowers listed on previous trails plus Trout Lily [Yellow Adder's Tongue] (few)

<u>Bluebird Trail to left (twice)</u>   *Early Season*: Violet (yellow), Trout Lily [Yellow Adder's Tongue] (very few)

Late Season: No flowers observed except Skunk Cabbage.

Arrowhead
See Trail Information for directions to Wildflower Garden.

<u>Wildflower Garden</u>. *Early Season*: Bloodroot (few), Siberian Scilla [Spring Squill], Daffodil

Canoe Meadows

<u>Sacred Way Trail</u> *See Trail Information for directions.*

Early Season: Bluets [Quaker Ladies, Innocence], Bloodroot, Trout Lily [Yellow Adder's Tongue] (many), Common Shadbush, Wake-robin [Birthroot, Purple or Red Trillium], Dutchman's Breeches, Wood Anemone [Windflower], Sessile-leaved Bellwort [Wild Oats], Violet (blue)

Late Season: Bloodroot (few)

<u>Road</u> *See Trail Information for directions.*

Early Season: Bloodroot, Siberian Scilla [Spring Squill], Myrtle [Periwinkle], Skunk Cabbage, Bluets [Quaker Ladies, Innocence], Wake-robin [Purple or Red Trillium], Sessile-leaved Bellwort [Wild Oats], Trout Lily [Yellow Adder's Tongue], Coltsfoot

Late Season: Bloodroot, Siberian Scilla [Spring Squill], Trout Lily [Yellow Adder's Tongue], Myrtle [Periwinkle] (beginning to bloom), Snowdrop [Early Snowdrop], Skunk Cabbage, Coltsfoot

<u>Wolf Pine Trail</u> *Early Season:* Some flowers listed along Road plus Marsh Marigold [Cowslip] (beginning to bloom), Carolina Spring Beauty, Japanese Spurge

Late Season: Coltsfoot, Skunk Cabbage, Bloodroot, Trout Lily [Yellow Adder's Tongue], Siberian Scilla [Spring Squill], Snowdrop [Early Snowdrop], Japanese Spurge

Trails across from Hancock Shaker Village
See Trail Information for directions.

<u>Road through Field</u>   *Early Season*: Bloodroot, Smooth Shadbush, Common Shadbush

Late Season: Bloodroot

<u>Road to right through woods</u>   *Early Season*: Wake-robin [Birthroot, Purple or Red Trillium] (many), Bloodroot (quite a few), Skunk Cabbage, Dutchman's Breeches (beginning to bloom), Carolina Spring Beauty (many), Trout Lily [Yellow Adder's Tongue] (few), Early Meadow Rue

Late Season: Bloodroot, Skunk Cabbage

FIRST TWO WEEKS IN MAY

Benedict Pond
See Trail Information for directions.

<u>Pond Loop Trail to left of swimming area</u>   *Early Season*:
Trout Lily [Yellow Adder's Tongue], Dwarf Ginseng (many),
Hobblebush (many - some near end of bloom), Golden
Alexanders (beginning to bloom), Sessile-leaved Bellwort
[Wild Oats] (quite a few), Early Low Blueberry (many),
Starflower (beginning to bloom), Wake-robin [Birthroot,
Purple or Red Trillium] (many), Hairy Solomon's Seal
(beginning to bloom), Bluets [Quaker Ladies, Innocence],
Toothwort [Crinkleroot] (many), Jack-in-the-pulpit [Indian
Turnip], Violet (light purple-few), Foamflower [False
Miterwort] (beginning to bloom), Highbush [Swamp]
Blueberry, Early Meadow Rue (near end of bloom),
Baneberry, Wild Geranium [Spotted Cranesbill] (beginning
to bloom), Apple, Marsh Marigold [Cowslip] (many),
Goldthread (many), Bunchberry [Dwarf Cornel] (beginning
to bloom)

Late Season: Trout Lily [Yellow Adder's Tongue], Carolina
Spring Beauty, Trailing Arbutus [Mayflower], Wake-robin
[Birthroot, Purple or Red Trillium] (beginning to bloom),
Sessile-leaved Bellwort [Wild Oats] (beginning to bloom),
Golden Alexanders (beginning to bloom), Marsh Marigold
[Cowslip] (beginning to bloom), Bluets [Quaker Ladies,
Innocence] (few)

Pleasant Valley

Path to Pike's Pond Trail   *See Trail Information for directions.*

Early Season: Red-berried Elder, Wild Strawberry, Bluets [Quaker Ladies, Innocence], Early Low Blueberry

Late Season: Forsythia, Daffodil, Virginia Bluebells [Virginia Cowslip], Smaller Forget-me-not

Pike's Pond Trail   *Early Season*: Some flowers observed on Path to Trail plus Morrow's Honeysuckle (beginning to bloom), Smaller Forget-me-not, Apple, Cuckooflower [Lady's Smock] (many), Golden Alexanders (beginning to bloom), Jack-in-the-pulpit [Indian Turnip], Toothwort [Crinkleroot], Wake-robin [Birthroot, Purple or Red Trillium], Foamflower [False Miterwort], Violet (white, yellow-many, medium blue), Goldthread, Sessile-leaved Bellwort [Wild Oats] (beginning to bloom), Marsh Marigold [Cowslip] (many near end of bloom)

Late Season: Bluets [Quaker Ladies, Innocence], Shadbush, Violet (purple), Trailing Arbutus [Mayflower], Sessile-leaved Bellwort [Wild Oats], Wake-robin [Birthroot, Purple or Red Trillium], Blue Cohosh (purplish colored), Wild Ginger, Hobblebush (one), Marsh Marigold [Cowslip] (many), Virginia Bluebells [Virginia Cowslip]

Path to Bluebird Trail   *See Trail Information for directions.*

Early Season: Red-berried Elder, Wild Strawberry, Bluets [Quaker Ladies, Innocence], Early Low Blueberry

Late Season: Forsythia, Daffodil, Polyanthus Primrose, Virginia Bluebells [Virginia Cowslip], Bugle, Ground Ivy [Gill-over-the-ground], Violet (white), Smaller Forget-me-not, Bluets [Quaker Ladies, Innocence], Canada Pussytoes

Bluebird Trail and entire loop *Early Season*: Violet (white, yellow, medium blue), Wake-robin [Birthroot, Purple or Red Trillium], Jack-in-the-pulpit [Indian Turnip], Cuckooflower [Lady's Smock], Wood Betony [Lousewort], Buttercup (beginning to bloom)

Bluebird Trail *Late Season:* No flowers were observed.

Yokun Trail to right *Late Season:* Wake-robin [Birthroot, Purple or Red Trillium], Marsh Marigold [Cowslip] (quite a few in one place), Violet (white), Smooth Shadbush, Bluets [Quaker Ladies, Innocence] (many in places), Common Shadbush

Old Wood Road to left *Late Season:* Bluets [Quaker Ladies, Innocence], Wood Betony [Lousewort], Early Low Blueberry

Beaver Lodge Trail to left *Late Season:* Smooth Shadbush (quite a few), Trout Lily [Yellow Adder's Tongue] (few), Cuckooflower [Lady's Smock], Early Low Blueberry (beginning to bloom), Bluets [Quaker Ladies, Innocence] (few)

Bluebird Trail to left (twice) *Late Season:* Violet (yellow)

Arrowhead
See Trail Information for directions to Wildflower Garden.

Wildflower Garden. *Early Season*: Baneberry, Crested Iris (beginning to bloom), Large-flowered Trillium, Woodruff, Wild Geranium [Spotted Cranesbill], Shooting Star (white), Wild Ginger, Great Solomon's Seal, Wake-robin [Birthroot, Purple or Red Trillium], Larger Yellow Lady's Slipper (beginning to bloom), Myrtle [Periwinkle], Lily-of-the-valley (beginning to bloom), Golden Alexanders

Late Season: Daffodil, Virginia Bluebells [Virginia Cowslip], Myrtle [Periwinkle] (many), Bloodroot (few), Siberian Scilla [Spring Squill]

Canoe Meadows

Sacred Way Trail   *See Trail Information for directions.*

Early Season: Bluets [Quaker Ladies, Innocence], Wild Strawberry, Cuckooflower [Lady's Smock] (many), Golden Alexanders (many), Violet (yellow, medium blue, white, purple, light blue), Apple (many), Bird [Pin, Fire] Cherry, Morrow's Honeysuckle (beginning to bloom), Hybrid of Morrow's and Tartarian Honeysuckle (beginning to bloom), Trout Lily [Yellow Adder's Tongue] (near end of bloom), Chokecherry, Wood Anemone [Windflower] (many), Sessile-leaved Bellwort [Wild Oats] (many), Wake-robin [Birthroot, Purple or Red Trillium] (many - near end of bloom), Blue Cohosh (near end of bloom), Early Low Blueberry, Foamflower [False Miterwort] (beginning to bloom), Japanese Barberry, Garden Currant, Common Winter Cress [Yellow Rocket]

Late Season: Trout Lily [Yellow Adder's Tongue] (quite a few), Bloodroot (few), Common Shadbush., Field Pussytoes (few), Smooth Shadbush (beginning to bloom), Sessile-leaved Bellwort [Wild Oats] (many), Wake-robin [Birthroot, Purple or Red Trillium], Wood Anemone [Windflower] (many), Violet (medium blue, light blue, small white,), Bluets [Quaker Ladies, Innocence], Blue Cohosh, Cuckooflower [Lady's Smock] (beginning to bloom)

Road   *See Trail Information for directions.*

Early Season: Lilac, Bluets [Quaker Ladies, Innocence], Cuckooflower [Lady's Smock], Violet (purple, white with deep blue center, yellow, white, medium blue), Myrtle [Periwinkle], Morrow's Honeysuckle (beginning to bloom), Hybrid of Morrow's and Tartarian Honeysuckle (beginning to bloom), Red-berried Elder, Wild Strawberry, Greek Valerian (beginning to bloom), Golden Alexanders (beginning to bloom), Chokecherry, Starflower (beginning to bloom), Goldthread (many), Painted Trillium (few), Trout Lily [Yellow Adder's Tongue] (near end of bloom), Sessile-leaved Bellwort [Wild Oats] (many), Wake-robin [Birthroot, Purple or Red Trillium], Foamflower [False Miterwort] (beginning to bloom), Japanese Barberry

Late Season: Bluets [Quaker Ladies, Innocence], Golden Alexanders (beginning to bloom), Bloodroot (quite a few), Myrtle [Periwinkle] (many), Siberian Scilla [Spring Squill] (near end of bloom), Violet (white with purple lines in center, purple, blue, yellow), Wild Strawberry (few), Skunk Cabbage (near end of bloom), Carolina Spring Beauty, Sessile-leaved Bellwort [Wild Oats] (many), Trout Lily [Yellow Adder's

Tongue] (few), Wake-robin [Birthroot, Purple or Red Trillium], Goldthread, Cuckooflower [Lady's Smock] (quite a few), Coltsfoot

<u>Wolf Pine Trail</u>   *Early Season*: Some flowers mentioned along road plus Dwarf Ginseng, Japanese Barberry, Marsh Marigold [Cowslip] (many - near end of bloom), Carolina Spring Beauty, Flowering Quince [Texas Scarlet Quince], Jack-in-the-pulpit [Indian Turnip] (beginning to bloom), Japanese Spurge

Late Season: Violet (purple, white), Bluets [Quaker Ladies, Innocence], Carolina Spring Beauty (few), Toothwort [Crinkleroot], Sessile-leaved Bellwort [Wild Oats] (many), Coltsfoot (one), Trout Lily [Yellow Adder's Tongue], Wake-robin [Birthroot, Purple or Red Trillium], Marsh Marigold [Cowslip] (beginning to bloom), Siberian Scilla [Spring Squill] (near end of bloom), Bloodroot (many), Japanese Spurge

Trails across from Hancock Shaker Village
See Trail Information for directions.

<u>Road through field</u>   *Early Season*: Wild Strawberry, Apple, Celandine, Chokecherry

Late Season: Bloodroot (few-in partially shaded area), Common Shadbush, Smooth Shadbush (beginning to bloom), Wild Strawberry (beginning to bloom)

<u>Road to right through woods</u>   *Early Season*: Ground Ivy [Gill-over-the-ground], Violet (yellow, purple, medium blue),

Wake-robin [Birthroot, Purple or Red Trillium] (near end of bloom), Jack-in-the-pulpit [Indian Turnip], Foamflower [False Miterwort], Wild Ginger, Sessile-leaved Bellwort [Wild Oats], Golden Alexanders, Hairy Solomon's Seal (beginning to bloom), Dutchman's Breeches (near end of bloom), Toothwort [Crinkleroot], Carolina Spring Beauty (near end of bloom), Miterwort [Bishop's Cap]

Late Season: Wake-robin [Birthroot, Purple or Red Trillium] (many), Bloodroot (near end of bloom), Early Meadow Rue (beginning to bloom), Jack-in-the-pulpit [Indian Turnip] (few-beginning to bloom), Blue Cohosh (few), Sessile-leaved Bellwort [Wild Oats] (beginning to bloom), Trout Lily [Yellow Adder's Tongue] (two), Violet (white, yellow - few) Carolina Spring Beauty (quite a few), Dutchman's Breeches (few)

<u>Road past field toward highway</u>   *Early Season*:   Common Winter Cress [Yellow Rocket]

Late Season: No flowers were observed.

LAST TWO WEEKS IN MAY

Benedict Pond
See Trail Information for directions.

<u>Path to Pond Loop Trail (beginning at left of swimming area)</u>
Late Season: Common Winter Cress [Yellow Rocket], Violet (light blue, dark blue - near end of bloom), Black Chokeberry, Pink Azalea [Pinxter Flower].

<u>Pond Loop Trail to left</u> *Early Season*: Pink Azalea [Pinxter Flower] (many in light shade), Starflower (quite a few), Cursed Crowfoot (several in places), Canada Mayflower [Wild Lily-of-the-valley] (many), Yellow Clintonia [Bluebead] (many), Highbush [Swamp] Blueberry, Wild Sarsaparilla (many in places), Dwarf Ginseng, Golden Alexanders, Wild Geranium [Spotted Cranesbill] (many in spots), Wake-robin [Birthroot, Purple or Red Trillium] (near end of bloom), Hairy Solomon's Seal, Jack-in-the-pulpit [Indian Turnip], Foamflower [False Miterwort], Buttercup, Larger Blue Flag Iris, Painted Trillium (few), Sessile-leaved Bellwort [Wild Oats] (few), Bunchberry [Dwarf Cornel], Bluets [Quaker Ladies, Innocence] (many)

Late Season: Pink Azalea [Pinxter Flower] (beginning to bloom - quite a few near pond), Starflower (quite a few), Canada Mayflower [Wild Lily-of-the-valley] (beginning to bloom - many in places), Foamflower [False Miterwort] (many in places), Yellow Clintonia [Bluebead] (many - beginning to bloom), Bluets [Quaker Ladies, Innocence] (few), Golden Alexanders (many in places), Wild Sarsaparilla (beginning to bloom), Highbush [Swamp] Blueberry, Wild Geranium [Spotted Cranesbill] (beginning to bloom), Early Low Blueberry (near end of bloom), Painted Trillium, Sessile-leaved Bellwort [Wild Oats], Jack-in-the-pulpit [Indian Turnip],

Violet (lilac color, purple, blue - near end of bloom), Cursed
Crowfoot, Small-flowered Crowfoot, Hairy Solomon's Seal,
Bellwort, Baneberry, Strawberry, Wake-robin [Birthroot,
Purple of Red Trillium] (near end of bloom), Buttercup, Marsh
Marigold [Cowslip] (near end of bloom), Dwarf Ginseng,
Toothwort {Crinkleroot] (near end of bloom), Bunchberry
[Dwarf Cornel] (beginning to bloom), Goldthread

Pleasant Valley

<u>Near Entrance</u>   *Early Season*: Lilac

<u>Path to Pike's Pond Trail</u>   *See Trail Information for directions.*

Early Season: Great Solomon's Seal, Morrow's Honeysuckle,
Lilac, Smaller Forget-me-not, Bleeding Heart

Late Season: Lily-of-the-valley, Smaller Forget-me-not,
Violet (purple), Lilac, Robin's Plantain, Bugle, Bleeding Heart,
Primrose, Jacob's Ladder, Virginia Bluebells [Virginia
Cowslip], Great Solomon's Seal, Bird's-eye [Germander]
Speedwell (many), Chokecherry, Ground Ivy [Gill-over-the-
ground] (many), Bluets [Quaker Ladies, Innocence] (many),
Common Winter Cress [Yellow Rocket] (few)

<u>Pike's Pond Trail</u>   *Early Season*: Bird's-eye [Germander]
Speedwell, Smaller Forget-me-not, Golden Alexanders,
Morrow's Honeysuckle, Jack-in-the-pulpit [Indian Turnip],
Wake-robin [Birthroot, Purple or Red Trillium] (near end of
bloom), Violet (medium blue, yellow- near end of bloom),
Cuckooflower [Lady's Smock] (near end of bloom),
Foamflower [False Miterwort], Robin's Plantain, Lily-of-the-
valley, Wild Strawberry, Pink Azalea [Pinxter Flower] (many),

Wild Geranium [Spotted Cranesbill] (beginning to bloom), Wild Sarsaparilla, Bluets [Quaker Ladies, Innocence], Starflower (many), Canada Mayflower [Wild Lily-of-the-valley] (many), Baneberry, Hairy Solomon's Seal (few), Yellow Clintonia [Bluebead] (few), Red-osier Dogwood, Buttercup, Dame's Violet [Dame's Rocket]

Late Season: Chokecherry, Smaller Forget-me-not, Bird's-eye [Germander] Speedwell, Cuckooflower [Lady's Smock], Marsh Marigold [Cowslip] (near end of bloom), Foamflower [False Miterwort], Robin's Plantain, Wild Geranium [Spotted Cranesbill] (beginning to bloom), Hairy Solomon's Seal, Starflower (beginning to bloom), Jack-in-the-pulpit [Indian Turnip], Violet (yellow, blue, purple), Golden Alexanders, Baneberry, Cattail, Hobblebush (one), Highbush [Swamp] Blueberry, Early Low Blueberry, Goldthread (near end of bloom), Canada Mayflower [Wild Lily-of-the-valley] (beginning to bloom), Lily-of-the-valley (beginning to bloom), Bluets [Quaker Ladies, Innocence], Strawberry, Japanese Barberry, Crab Apple

Path to Bluebird Trail
See Trail Information for directions.

Lily-of-the-valley, Smaller Forget-me-not, Violet (purple), Lilac, Robin's Plantain, Bugle, Bleeding Heart, Primrose, Jacob's Ladder, Virginia Bluebells [Virginia Cowslip], Great Solomon's Seal, Bird's-eye [Germander] Speedwell (many), Chokecherry, Ground Ivy [Gill-over-the-ground] (many), Bluets [Quaker Ladies, Innocence] (many), Common Winter Cress [Yellow Rocket], Canada Pussytoes

Bluebird Trail   *Early Season*: Golden Alexanders, Canada Mayflower [Wild Lily-of-the-valley], Morrow's Honeysuckle, Wild Strawberry, Bluets [Quaker Ladies, Innocence]

Late Season: Bluets [Quaker Ladies, Innocence] (many in places), Golden Alexanders, Strawberry

Yokun Trail to right   *Early Season*: Some flowers observed on the Bluebird Trail plus Foamflower [False Miterwort], Violet (yellow, blue), Baneberry, Jack-in-the-pulpit [Indian Turnip], Starflower, Spatterdock [Yellow Pond Lily, Cow Lily], Cuckooflower [Lady's Smock]

Late Season: Violet (purple, blue, yellow), Jack-in-the-pulpit [Indian Turnip], Baneberry (beginning to bloom), Starflower, Early Low Blueberry, Cuckooflower [Lady's Smock], Chokecherry (near end of bloom)

Old Wood Road to left   *Early Season*: Some flowers listed on Bluebird and Yokun Trails plus Red-osier Dogwood, Blue-eyed Grass (beginning to bloom), Golden Ragwort (near end of bloom), Jack-in-the-pulpit [Indian Turnip], Wood Strawberry (few), Common Cinquefoil (beginning to bloom), Cursed Crowfoot (near end of bloom), Baneberry, Miterwort [Bishop's Cap] (few), Wild Ginger, Violet (yellow)

Late Season: Canada Mayflower [Wild Lily-of-the-valley] (beginning to bloom), Wood Betony [Lousewort], Bluets [Quaker Ladies, Innocence] (many), Strawberry, Jack-in-the-pulpit [Indian Turnip], Cream-colored Avens

Beaver Lodge Trail to left   *Late Season:* Chokecherry, Morrow's Honeysuckle (beginning to bloom), Cuckooflower

[Lady's Smock], Hawthorn, Early Low Blueberry, Bluets [Quaker Ladies, Innocence], Starflower

<u>Bluebird Trail to left (twice)</u>   *Early Season*: Starflower, Jack-in-the-pulpit [Indian Turnip]

Late Season: Violet, (light violet with dark violet lines in center, yellow), Wake-robin [Birthroot, Purple or Red Trillium] (one)

Arrowhead
See Trail Information for directions to Wildflower Garden.

<u>Entrance</u>   *Early Season*: Lilac, Morrow's Honeysuckle

<u>Wildflower Garden</u>.   *Early Season*: Red-osier Dogwood, Wild Geranium [Spotted Cranesbill], Jacob's Ladder, Golden Alexanders, Garden Lupine, Herb Robert, Crested Iris (near end of bloom), False Solomon's Seal [Wild Spikenard], Large-flowered Trillium (near end of bloom), Shooting Star (white-near end of bloom), Garden [European] Columbine, Mayapple [Mandrake], Great Solomon's Seal, Lily-of-the-valley, Larger Yellow Lady's Slipper (near end of bloom), Rhododendron (yellow and dark rose), Myrtle (Periwinkle), Baneberry

Late Season: Crested Iris, Jacob's Ladder, Large Flowered Trillium, Shooting Star (white), Virginia Bluebells [Virginia Cowslip], Baneberry, Myrtle [Periwinkle], Violet (yellow), Toad Trillium [Toadshade], Rue Anemone, Larger Yellow Lady's Slipper, Great Solomon's Seal, Golden Alexanders, Wake-robin [Birthroot, Purple or Red Trillium]

Canoe Meadows

Sacred Way Trail   *See Trail Information for directions.*

Early Season: Morrow's Honeysuckle, Hybrid of Morrow's and Tartarian Honeysuckle] (many), Common Cinquefoil (many), Bluets [Quaker Ladies, Innocence] (many), Golden Alexanders (many in places), Buttercup, Red-osier Dogwood (many), Common Winter Cress [Yellow Rocket] (many), Dame's Violet [Dame's Rocket] (white and lilac- many in places), Wild Strawberry, Common [Philadelphia] Fleabane, Hawthorn, Canada Mayflower [Wild Lily-of-the-valley] (many), Wild Sarsaparilla, False Solomon's Seal [Wild Spikenard] (beginning to bloom), Foamflower [False Miterwort], Blue-eyed Grass (one), Cuckooflower [Lady's Smock] (near end of bloom)

Late Season: Bluets [Quaker Ladies, Innocence], Golden Alexanders (many in places), Strawberry, Common Winter Cress [Yellow Rocket], Dame's Violet [Dame's Rocket] (beginning to bloom), Cuckooflower [Lady's Smock] (many in places - near end of bloom), Morrow's Honeysuckle, Robin's Plantain, Hybrid of Morrow's and Tartarian Honeysuckle, Dwarf Cinquefoil, Apple (near end of bloom), Chokecherry, Sessile-leaved Bellwort [Wild Oats], Wild Sarsaparilla, Canada Mayflower [Wild Lily-of-the-valley] (quite a few), Hairy Solomon's Seal, Foamflower [False Miterwort}, Violet (lilac color), Buttercup

Road   *See Trail Information for directions.*

Early Season: Bluets [Quaker Ladies, Innocence], Shepherd's Purse, Buttercup (many in places), Morrow's Honeysuckle, Golden Alexanders (many), Myrtle (Periwinkle), Violet (purple, white with blue center, medium blue, light blue), Baneberry, Red-berried Elder, Greek Valerian, Wood Strawberry, Dame's Violet [Dame's Rocket] (white- beginning to bloom), Canada Anemone (beginning to bloom), Wild Sarsaparilla (many in places), Bunchberry [Dwarf Cornel] (few), Starflower, Common Cinquefoil, Canada Mayflower [Wild Lily-of-the-valley] (many in spots), Red-osier Dogwood (many), Highbush Cranberry (few), Pink Azalea [Pinxter Flower] (few), Cuckooflower [Lady's Smock] (near end of bloom), Painted Trillium (one), False Solomon's Seal [Wild Spikenard] (beginning to bloom), Hybrid of Tartarian and Morrow's Honeysuckle, Ragged Robin [Cuckooflower], Common [Philadelphia] Fleabane

Late Season: Golden Alexanders, Violet (blue, purple, yellow, white), Myrtle [Periwinkle], Red-berried Elder, Lilac, Greek Valerian, Wake-robin [Birthroot, Purple or Red Trillium] (near end of bloom), Canada Mayflower [Wild Lily-of-the-valley], Starflower, Nodding Trillium, Yellow Clintonia [Bluebead)] (starting to bloom), Strawberry, Foamflower [False Miterwort], Cuckooflower [Lady's Smock], Goldthread, Rosybells [Rose Twisted Stalk or Rose Mandarin] (few), Marsh Marigold [Cowslip] (near end of bloom), Common [Philadelphia] Fleabane, Red Baneberry, Morrow's Honeysuckle, Hybrid of Morrow's and Tartarian Honeysuckle, Crab Apple, Highbush [Swamp] Blueberry

<u>Wolf Pine Trail</u> *Early Season*: Some flowers listed on the road plus Cursed Crowfoot, Marsh Marigold [Cowslip] (near end of bloom), Wild Ginger (few), Bluets [Quaker Ladies, Innocence], Indian Cucumber Root, Lilac, Flowering Quince [Texas Scarlet Quince], Japanese Barberry, Jack-in-the-pulpit [Indian Turnip], Wild Strawberry, Yellow Clintonia [Bluebead] (many in spots)

Trails across from Hancock Shaker Village
See Trail Information for directions.

Road through field   *Early Season*: Mayapple [Mandrake]
(in shade- quite a few), Common Cinquefoil, Lesser
Stitchwort, Hawthorn

Late Season: Chokecherry, Apple (near end of bloom),
Golden Alexanders, Strawberry, Celandine, Common Winter
Cress [Yellow Rocket], Field Pansy, Early Low Blueberry,
Bird [Pin, Fire] Cherry, Smaller Forget-me-not

Road to right through woods   *Early Season*: Jack-in-the-
pulpit [Indian Turnip], Canada Mayflower, [Wild Lily-of-the-
valley], Aniseroot, Common Blackberry (beginning to bloom),
Golden Alexanders, Celandine, False Solomon's Seal [Wild
Spikenard], Baneberry, Foamflower [False Miterwort],
Common Winter Cress [Yellow Rocket], Hairy Solomon's
Seal (near end of bloom), Yellow Clintonia [Bluebead], Indian
Cucumber Root (beginning to bloom)

Late Season: Common Winter Cress [Yellow Rocket],
Golden Alexanders (many in spots), Ground Ivy [Gill-over-
the-ground], Red Baneberry, Jack-in-the-pulpit [Indian
Turnip], Wake-robin [Birthroot, Purple or Red Trillium]
(many), Cream-colored Avens, Starflower, Toothwort
[Crinkleroot], Foamflower [False Miterwort] (many in places),
Hairy Solomon's Seal, Violet (purple), Yellow Clintonia
[Bluebead] (beginning to bloom), Miterwort, [Bishop's Cap]

<u>Path partway around Shaker reservoir</u>:   *Early Season*:
Common Cinquefoil, Blue-eyed Grass (few), Robin's Plantain,
Buttercup, Field Hawkweed [King Devil], Common
Blackberry, False Solomon's Seal [Wild Spikenard], Highbush
[Swamp] Blueberry, Common Winter Cress [Yellow Rocket]

Late Season: Early Low Blueberry, Chokecherry, Highbush
[Swamp] Blueberry, Robin's Plantain (many in one spot),
Morrow's Honeysuckle, Golden Alexanders, Blue-eyed Grass
(beginning to bloom), Smooth Shadbush (near end of bloom),
Strawberry

<u>Road to Highway</u> *Early Season*: Highbush Cranberry

Late Season: Violet (purple), Golden Alexanders, Common
Winter Cress [Yellow Rocket], Apple (near end of bloom),
Chokecherry

FIRST TWO WEEKS IN JUNE

Benedict Pond
See Trail Information for directions.

<u>Path to Pond Loop Trail (beginning at left of swimming area)</u>
Late Season: Spiraea, Rhododendron (both in front of comfort facility - beginning to bloom), Round-leaved Dogwood, Pink Azalea [Pinxter Flower]

<u>Pond Loop Trail to left</u> *Early Season*: Highbush Cranberry, Common Blackberry, Field Hawkweed [King Devil], Pink Azalea [Pinxter Flower] (near end of bloom - many in places), Maple-leaved Viburnum [Dockmackie], Canada Mayflower [Wild Lily-of-the-valley] (near end of bloom), False Solomon s Seal [Wild Spikenard] (near end of bloom), Arrowwood (beginning to bloom), Sweet-scented Water Lily (white - beginning to bloom), Indian Cucumber Root, False [White] Hellebore [Indian Poke], Aniseroot, Wild Geranium [Spotted Cranesbill] (many in places - near end of bloom), Buttercup, Common [Philadelphia] Fleabane, Robin s Plantain, Common Cinquefoil, Golden Alexanders (near end of bloom), Mountain Laurel (beginning to bloom), Bunchberry [Dwarf Cornel] (quite a few), Starflower (near end of bloom), Sweet Viburnum [Nannyberry], Bluets [Quaker Ladies, Innocence], Rattlesnake Weed

Late Season: Red-osier Dogwood (by pond), Arrowwood, False Solomon s Seal [Wild Spikenard], Canada Mayflower [Wild Lily-of-the-valley] (many), Yellow Clintonia [Bluebead] (many), Starflower, Pink Azalea [Pinxter Flower] (quite a few near pond), Golden Alexanders, Wild Sarsaparilla, Black Chokeberry, Common Winter Cress [Yellow Rocket], Wild Geranium [Spotted Cranesbill] (many near pond and by wide area of trail), Golden Ragwort (many near pond), Spatterdock [Yellow Pond Lily, Cow Lily], Indian Cucumber Root, Early Low Blueberry, Jack-in-the-pulpit [Indian Turnip], White Baneberry [Doll's Eyes], False [White] Hellebore [Indian Poke], Hairy Solomon's Seal, Aniseroot (many in places), Robin's Plantain, Violet (blue - one), Foamflower [False Miterwort], Cream-colored Avens, Highbush Cranberry, Buttercup, Highbush [Swamp] Blueberry, Bunchberry [Dwarf Cornel], Bluets [Quaker Ladies, Innocence]

Pleasant Valley

<u>Near entrance</u> *Early Season*: Mountain Laurel

<u>Path to Pike's Pond Trail including wildflower garden</u>
See Trail Information for directions.

Early Season: Smaller Forget-me-not, Garden Valerian [Garden Heliotrope] (beginning to bloom), Dame's Violet [Dame's Rocket] (near end of bloom), Buttercup (quite a few), Bird's-eye Primrose, Wild Columbine, Ground Ivy [Gill-over-the-ground], Wild Radish, Common Cinquefoil, Rough Cinquefoil, Common Blackberry, Golden Alexanders (near end of bloom)

Late Season: Apple, Smaller Forget-me-not, Dame's Violet [Dame's Rocket], Wild Columbine, Bird's-eye Primrose, Common Winter Cress [Yellow Rocket], Buttercup, Great Solomon's Seal, Bluets [Quaker Ladies, Innocence], Common Cinquefoil, Wild Radish, Lesser Stitchwort

Pike's Pond Trail   *Early Season*: Common Cinquefoil, Smaller Forget-me-not (near end of bloom), Buttercup, Maiden Pink, Common Blackberry (many), Orange Hawkweed [Devil's Paintbrush], Highbush Cranberry, Dame's Violet [Dame's Rocket] (near end of bloom), Bird's-eye [Germander] Speedwell, Golden Alexanders (near end of bloom), Field Hawkweed [King Devil], Wild Geranium [Spotted Cranesbill], Round-leaved Ragwort (near end of bloom), Arrowwood (beginning to bloom), Robin's Plantain, Larger Blue Flag Iris, Blue-eyed Grass, Dwarf Cinquefoil, Maple-leaved Viburnum [Dockmackie], Mountain Laurel (beginning to bloom - many), False Solomon's Seal [Wild Spikenard] (near end of bloom), Common [Philadelphia] Fleabane (few), Spatterdock [Yellow Pond Lily, Cow Lily] (few), Yellow Iris (few), Bittersweet Nightshade, Bluets [Quaker Ladies, Innocence]

Late Season: Common Cinquefoil, Bluets [Quaker Ladies, Innocence], Strawberry, Morrow's Honeysuckle (near end of bloom), Spatterdock [Yellow Pond Lily, Cow Lily], Red-osier Dogwood, Smaller Forget-me-not, False Solomon's Seal [Wild Spikenard], Robin's Plantain, Lily-of-the-valley, Wild Sarsaparilla, Jack-in-the-pulpit [Indian Turnip], Canada Mayflower [Wild Lily-of-the-valley] (few), Bird's-eye [Germander] Speedwell, Common Blackberry, Dame's Violet [Dame's Rocket], Wild Geranium [Spotted Cranesbill], Violet, Foamflower [False Miterwort], Cuckooflower [Lady's Smock], Golden Ragwort, Larger Blue Flag Iris (beginning to bloom), Common [Philadelphia] Fleabane, Pink Azalea [Pinxter Flower], Buttercup, Highbush Cranberry

Honeysuckle Lane *See Trail Information for directions.*

Early Season: Dame's Violet [Dame's Rocket], Smaller Forget-me-not, Buttercup (quite a few), Ragged Robin [Cuckooflower] (one), Yellow Avens

Late Season: Dame's Violet [Dame's Rocket], Smaller Forget-me-not, Buttercup, Common Winter Cress [Yellow Rocket], Red-osier Dogwood, Morrow's Honeysuckle, Bird's-eye [Germander] Speedwell (near end of bloom), Highbush Cranberry

Bluebird Trail, Yokun Trail, Old Wood Road, Beaver Lodge Trail, and Bluebird Trail *See Trail Information for directions.*

Early Season: Robin's Plantain, Buttercup, Common Cinquefoil, Golden Alexanders (near end of bloom), Yarrow [Milfoil] (beginning to bloom), Common Blackberry, Bluets [Quaker Ladies, Innocence], Whorled [Four-leaved] Loosestrife (beginning to bloom), Maple-leaved Viburnum [Dockmackie] (many), Jack-in-the-pulpit [Indian Turnip] (near end of bloom), Arrowwood (many), Spatterdock [Yellow Pond Lily, Cow Lily], Bush Honeysuckle, Field Hawkweed [King Devil] (many in one place), Orange Hawkweed [Devil's Paintbrush], Smaller Forget-me-not (near end of bloom), Larger Blue Flag Iris, Cuckooflower [Lady's Smock] (near end of bloom), Asiatic Bittersweet, Mountain Laurel (quite a few), Common Speedwell, Tall Meadow Rue (one), Canada Mayflower [Wild Lily-of-the-valley] (near end of bloom)

Bluebird Trail *Late Season*: Golden Alexanders, Morrow's Honeysuckle, Bluets [Quaker Ladies, Innocence] (many), Wild Strawberry, Common Cinquefoil (few)

Yokun Trail to right   *Late Season*: Bluets [Quaker Ladies, Innocence] (many), Cinquefoil, Spatterdock [Yellow Pond Lily, Cow Lily], Jack-in-the-pulpit [Indian Turnip], Baneberry, False Solomon's Seal [Wild Spikenard], White Baneberry [Doll's Eyes], Golden Alexanders, Canada Mayflower [Wild Lily-of-the-valley], Cuckooflower [Lady's Smock] (few)

Old Wood Road to left   *Late Season*: Jack-in-the-pulpit [Indian Turnip], False Solomon's Seal [Wild Spikenard], Pink Azalea [Pinxter Flower] (quite a few), Wood Betony [Lousewort], Morrow's Honeysuckle (near end of bloom), Canada Mayflower [Wild Lily-of-the-valley], Bluets [Quaker Ladies, Innocence], Buttercup, Red-osier Dogwood

Beaver Lodge Trail to left   *Late Season*: Bluets [Quaker Ladies, Innocence], False Solomon's Seal [Wild Spikenard], White Baneberry [Doll's Eyes], Canada Mayflower [Wild Lily-of-the-valley], Pink Lady's Slipper [Moccasin Flower], Pink Azalea [Pinxter Flower], Morrow's Honeysuckle, Jack-in-the-pulpit [Indian Turnip], Buttercup, Golden Ragwort (many in one spot)

Bluebird Trail to left (twice) *Late Season:* Canada Mayflower [Wild Lily-of-the-valley] (few)

West Mountain Road (Pleasant Valley Property)
Early Season: Yellow Iris, Arrowwood

Late Season: Yellow Iris, Highbush Cranberry

Arrowhead
See Trail Information for directions to Wildflower Garden.

Wildflower Garden: *Early Season*: Canada Anemone,
Rugosa Rose, Bladder Campion, Herb Robert, Garden
Lupine, Multiflora Rose, Garden [European] Columbine,
Oxeye Daisy, Baneberry, Robin's Plantain

Late Season: False Solomon's Seal [Wild Spikenard], Wild
Geranium [Spotted Cranesbill], Larger Yellow Lady's Slipper
(near end of bloom), Rugosa Rose (beginning to bloom), Red-
osier Dogwood, Garden [European] Columbine, Golden
Alexanders, Herb Robert, Garden Lupine, Wild Blue Phlox,
Toad Trillium [Toadshade], Wild Ginger, Garden Valerian
[Garden Heliotrope], Robin's Plantain, Great Solomon's Seal,
Bird's-eye [Germander] Speedwell, Lily-of-the-valley (white
and pink), Common [Philadelphia] Fleabane, Baneberry,
Rhododendron (yellow and dark rose), Common Winter Cress
[Yellow Rocket]

Area to left of Wildflower Garden   *Late Season*: Canada
Anemone, White Campion, Dame's Violet [Dame's Rocket]

Beside Exit Road   *Early Season*: Mountain Laurel

Canoe Meadows

Sacred Way Trail   *See Trail Information for directions.*

Early Season: Cow [Tufted] Vetch, Common Cinquefoil
(many in places), Yarrow [Milfoil], Dewberry, Bluets [Quaker

Ladies, Innocence], Maiden Pink, Orange Hawkweed [Devil's Paintbrush], Blue-eyed grass, Buttercup, Yellow Iris, Bittersweet Nightshade, Common Winter Cress [Yellow Rocket] (near end of bloom), Golden Alexanders, Dame's Violet [Dame's Rocket] (white, violet - many in places), Lesser Stitchwort, Common Blackberry, Common [Philadelphia] Fleabane, Morrow's Honeysuckle (near end of bloom), Arrowwood (beginning to bloom), Wild Strawberry, Spatterdock [Yellow Pond Lily, Cow Lily], Canada Mayflower [Wild Lily-of-the-valley] (many in places - some near end of bloom), One-flowered Cancerroot [Ghost Pipe], Red-osier Dogwood (near end of bloom), Cuckooflower [Lady's Smock] (near end of bloom), Larger Blue Flag Iris

Late Season: Indian Hemp, Golden Alexanders (many), Chokecherry, Common Cinquefoil (many), Cow [Tufted] Vetch, Blue-eyed Grass, Dewberry, Red-osier Dogwood, Watercress, Smaller Forget-me-not, Common Winter Cress [Yellow Rocket] (many), Dame's Violet [Dame's Rocket] (white, lilac, light lilac - many), Morrow's Honeysuckle, Hybrid of Morrow's and Tartarian Honeysuckle, Bluets [Quaker Ladies, Innocence], Canada Mayflower [Wild Lily-of-the-valley] (many), Buttercup, Strawberry, Robin's Plantain, Hawthorn (near end of bloom), Spatterdock [Yellow Pond Lily, Cow Lily], False Solomon's Seal [Wild Spikenard], Starflower (few), , Cuckooflower [Lady's Smock] (near end of bloom), Crab Apple, Canada Anemone, Maiden Pink, Common Blackberry, Bladder Campion, White Campion, Yellow Iris, Yellow Goatsbeard

Road   *See Trail Information for directions.*

Early Season: Lesser Stitchwort, Cow [Tufted] Vetch,
Yarrow [Milfoil], Hoary Alyssum, Bluets [Quaker Ladies,
Innocence], Silvery Cinquefoil, Bladder Campion, Maiden
Pink, White Campion, Morrow's Honeysuckle (near end of
bloom), Golden Alexanders, Thimbleberry [Black Raspberry]
(near end of bloom), Buttercup (many in places), Dame's
Violet [Dame's Rocket] (white, pink, lilac-many in places),
Day Lily (yellow), Canada Anemone, Common Cinquefoil,
Common Blackberry, Highbush Cranberry (near end of
bloom), Arrowwood (beginning to bloom), Pink Azalea
[Pinxter Flower] (near end of bloom - one), Indian Cucumber
Root, Dewberry, Robin's Plantain (few), Ragged Robin
[Cuckooflower] (many in places), Blue-eyed Grass (few),
Common [Philadelphia] Fleabane

Late Season: Cow [Tufted] Vetch, Hoary Alyssum, Lesser
Stitchwort, Silvery Cinquefoil (many), Yarrow [Milfoil]
(beginning to bloom), Common Cinquefoil, Bluets [Quaker
Ladies, Innocence], Dewberry, Morrow's Honeysuckle (near
end of bloom), Buttercup, White Campion (beginning to
bloom), Golden Alexanders, Shepherd's Purse, Hybrid of
Morrow's and Tartarian Honeysuckle (near end of bloom),
Violet (purple), Greek Valerian, Dame's Violet [Dame's
Rocket] (purple, violet, white - many), Canada Anemone
(beginning to bloom), Field Hawkweed [King Devil], Painted
Trillium (one), Starflower, Common Wood Sorrel (one), Pink
Lady's Slipper [Moccasin Flower] (one), Foamflower [False
Miterwort] (near end of bloom), Wild Sarsaparilla, Indian
Cucumber Root, Cuckooflower [Lady's Smock] (near end
of bloom), Common [Philadelphia] Fleabane, Blue-eyed Grass,

Swamp Dewberry, Canada Mayflower, [Wild Lily-of-the-valley], Starflower, Yellow Clintonia [Bluebead], Ragged Robin [Cuckooflower], Myrtle [Periwinkle], Highbush Cranberry, Red-osier Dogwood, Pink Azalea [Pinxter Flower], Bunchberry [Dwarf Cornel] (few)

<u>Wolf Pine Trail</u>   *Early Season*: Some flowers listed along road plus Canada Mayflower [Wild Lily-of-the-valley], Indian Cucumber Root, Lilac, Jack-in-the-pulpit [Indian Turnip] (near end of bloom)

Late Season: Cuckooflower [Lady's Smock] (near end of bloom), Morrow's Honeysuckle (near end of bloom), Common [Philadelphia] Fleabane, Bluets [Quaker Ladies, Innocence], Dwarf Cinquefoil, Starflower, Canada Mayflower [Wild Lily-of-the-valley] (many), Common Cinquefoil, Golden Alexanders, Bunchberry [Dwarf Cornel], Dame's Violet [Dame's Rocket] (mostly white), Indian Cucumber Root, Wild Strawberry, Wood Strawberry, Lilac, Wild Sarsaparilla, Violet (light purple, medium blue), Buttercup (few), Foamflower [False Miterwort], Jack-in-the-pulpit [Indian Turnip], Yellow Clintonia [Bluebead] (one - near end of bloom), Hybrid of Tartarian and Morrow's Honeysuckle (near end of bloom), False Solomon's Seal [Wild Spikenard]

Trails across from Hancock Shaker Village
See Trail Information for directions.

<u>Road through field</u>   *Early Season*: Field Hawkweed [King Devil] (many), Orange Hawkweed [Devil's Paintbrush], Lesser Stitchwort, Common Cinquefoil, Common Blackberry (near end of bloom), Tall Meadow Rue, Yarrow [Milfoil] (beginning to bloom), Buttercup (few)

Late Season: Common Cinquefoil (many), Field Hawkweed [King Devil] (many), Robin's Plantain, Chokecherry, Chokeberry, Mayapple [Mandrake], Apple, Tartarian Honeysuckle (near end of bloom), Celandine, Round-leaved Dogwood, Morrow's Honeysuckle, Common Winter Cress [Yellow Rocket] (near end of bloom), Lesser Stitchwort (many), Yarrow [Milfoil] (beginning to bloom), Wild Radish (few), Golden Alexanders, Common Speedwell, Blue-eyed Grass (few), Orange Hawkweed [Devil's Paintbrush] (few - beginning to bloom), Smaller Forget-me-not, Common Blackberry

<u>Road to right through woods</u>   *Early Season*: Celandine (near end of bloom), Ground Ivy [Gill-over-the-ground], Golden Alexanders (near end of bloom), Maple-leaved Viburnum [Dockmackie] (beginning to bloom), Great Angelica, Virginia Waterleaf (white and lavender), Indian Cucumber Root, Jack-in-the-pulpit [Indian Turnip] (near end of bloom)

Late Season: Common Winter Cress [Yellow Rocket], Strawberry, Ground Ivy [Gill-over-the-ground], Hawthorn, Common Blackberry, White Baneberry, Golden Ragwort, Violet (purple), Aniseroot, Golden Alexanders (many), Chokecherry, Tartarian Honeysuckle, False Solomon's Seal

[Wild Spikenard] (many), Canada Mayflower [Wild Lily-of-the-valley], Great Angelica, Jack-in-the-pulpit [Indian Turnip] (many), Foamflower [False Miterwort] (many), Wild Ginger, Red Baneberry, Starflower, Yellow Clintonia [Bluebead], Miterwort [Bishop's Cap]

Road past field toward highway *Early Season*: Arrowwood, Common Speedwell

Late Season: Strawberry, Common Blackberry, Round-leaved Dogwood, Buttercup, Golden Alexanders, Common Winter Cress [Yellow Rocket]

Path partway around Shaker reservoir *Late Season*: Tall Meadow Rue (beginning to bloom), Field Hawkweed [King Devil], Common Blackberry (quite a few), Buttercup, Early Low Blueberry, Morrow's Honeysuckle, Blue-eyed Grass (many in spots), Orange Hawkweed [Devil's Paintbrush] (beginning to bloom), Robin's Plantain, Red-osier Dogwood, False Solomon's Seal [Wild Spikenard], Common Cinquefoil, Golden Alexanders, Common [Philadelphia] Fleabane

Road to highway (continued) *Late Season*: Golden Alexanders, Common Blackberry, Highbush Cranberry (beginning to bloom), Buttercup

LAST TWO WEEKS IN JUNE

Benedict Pond
See Trail Information for directions.

<u>Path to Pond Loop Trail (beginning at left of swimming area)</u>
Early Season: Purple-flowering Raspberry, Yarrow [Milfoil], Mountain Laurel (many in various places around pond), Whorled [Four-leaved] Loosestrife (many here and around pond), Spreading Dogbane (beginning to bloom), Cowwheat (many here and around pond), Bladder Campion, Bush Honeysuckle

Late Season: Spiraea (near end of bloom), Rhododendron (both in front of comfort facility), Buttercup, Common Blackberry, Yarrow [Milfoil] (beginning to bloom), Lesser Stitchwort, Common Speedwell, Common Cinquefoil, Bush Honeysuckle, Field Hawkweed [King Devil]

<u>Pond Loop Trail to left</u>   *Early Season*: Some flowers listed on Path to Pond Loop Trail plus Swamp Dewberry, Wintergreen [Checkerberry] (many in spots), Indian Pipe [Corpse Plant], Sweet-scented Water Lily (white), Tall Meadow Rue, Arrowwood (near end of bloom), Larger Blue Flag Iris, Common Elder (quite a few near pond), Indian Cucumber Root, White Avens (few), Ragged Robin [Cuckooflower] (near end of bloom), Common [Philadelphia] Fleabane (near end of bloom), Buttercup, Daisy Fleabane [Sweet Scabious], Field Hawkweed [King Devil], Bluets [Quaker Ladies, Innocence]

Late Season: Mountain Laurel (many near pond), Pink Azalea
[Pinxter flower] (near end of bloom), Common Blackberry,
Yarrow [Milfoil], Wintergreen [Checkerberry] (beginning to
bloom), Maple-leaved Viburnum [Dockmackie], Cowwheat,
Canada Mayflower [Wild Lily-of-the-valley] (quite a few),
False Solomon's Seal [Wild Spikenard] (few - near end of
bloom), Indian Cucumber Root, Tall Meadow Rue,
Arrowwood, Spatterdock [Yellow Pond Lily, Cow Lily], False
[White] Hellebore [Indian Poke], Golden Alexanders,
Highbush Cranberry, Aniseroot (near end of bloom), Wild
Geranium [Spotted Cranesbill], Common Cinquefoil,
Common [Philadelphia] Fleabane, Buttercup, Purple-
flowering Raspberry (beginning to bloom), Larger Blue Flag
Iris, Bunchberry [Dwarf Cornel], Field Hawkweed [King
Devil] (many in one place), Orange Hawkweed [Devil's
Paintbrush] (many in one place), Mouse Ear, Bluets [Quaker
Ladies, Innocence]

Pleasant Valley

<u>Near Entrance</u>: *Early Season*: Mountain. Laurel

<u>Path to Pike's Pond Trail including wildflower garden</u>
See Trail Information for directions.

Late Season: Smaller Forget-me-not, Garden Valerian
[Garden Heliotrope], Dame's Violet [Dame's Rocket] (near
end of bloom), Buttercup (quite a few), Bird's-eye Primrose,
Wild Columbine, Ground Ivy [Gill-over-the-ground], Wild
Radish, Common Cinquefoil, Rough Cinquefoil, Common
Blackberry, Golden Alexanders (near end of bloom)

<u>Pike's Pond Trail</u>   *Early Season*: Buttercup, Maiden Pink, Meadowsweet, Field Hawkweed [King Devil], Orange Hawkweed [Devil's Paintbrush], Common Blackberry (near end of bloom), Wild Geranium [Spotted Cranesbill] (near end of bloom), Arrowwood (near end of bloom), Cuckooflower [Lady's Smock] (near end of bloom), Multiflora Rose (near end of bloom), Blue-eyed Grass, Robin's Plantain (near end of bloom), Common Cinquefoil, Mountain Laurel (many - full bloom), Smaller Forget-me-not (few - near end of bloom), Dame's Violet [Dame's Rocket] (near end of bloom), Garden Valerian [Garden Heliotrope]

Late Season: Jack-in-the-pulpit [Indian Turnip], Mountain Laurel, Dame's Violet [Dame's Rocket], Yellow Iris, Smaller Forget-me-not, Wild Geranium [Spotted Cranesbill], Common Blackberry, Bird's-eye [Germander] Speedwell, Ragwort, Field Hawkweed [King Devil], Robin's Plantain, Blue-eyed Grass, Dwarf Cinquefoil, Bluets [Quaker Ladies, Innocence], Maple-leaved Viburnum [Dockmackie] (one), Garden Valerian [Garden Heliotrope] (beginning to bloom), Larger Blue Flag Iris, Buttercup (quite a few), Highbush Cranberry (near end of bloom)

<u>Honeysuckle Lane</u>   *See Trail Information for directions*

Late Season: Dame's Violet [Dame's Rocket], Smaller Forget-me-not (many), Buttercup (quite a few), Ragged Robin [Cuckooflower] (one), Yellow Avens, Common Cinquefoil, Wild Radish

Path to Bluebird Trail   *See Trail Information for directions.*

Early Season: Field Hawkweed [King Devil], Orange Hawkweed [Devil's Paintbrush], Bluets [Quaker Ladies, Innocence], Yarrow [Milfoil]

Late Season: Smaller Forget-me-not, Garden Valerian [Garden Heliotrope], Dame's Violet [Dame's Rocket], Bird's-eye Primrose, Buttercup, Common Cinquefoil, Common Speedwell, Wild Radish (many), Field Hawkweed [King Devil] (beginning to bloom), Orange Hawkweed [Devil's Paintbrush] (beginning to bloom), Silvery Cinquefoil, Bladder Campion, Yarrow [Milfoil], Lesser Stitchwort, Bluets [Quaker Ladies, Innocence], Common Blackberry (near end of bloom), Larger Blue Flag Iris

Bluebird Trail   *Early Season*: Robin's Plantain, Yarrow [Milfoil], Orange Hawkweed [Devil's Paintbrush] (many), Common Cinquefoil, Whorled [Four-leaved] Loosestrife (many)

Late Season: Wild Radish, Orange Hawkweed [Devil's Paintbrush] (beginning to bloom), Yarrow [Milfoil], Buttercup, Common Blackberry (near end of bloom), Bluets [Quaker Ladies, Innocence], Whorled [Four-leaved] Loosestrife, Common Cinquefoil

Yokun Trail to right   *Early Season*: Some flowers listed on Path or Bluebird Trail plus Bush Honeysuckle, Maleberry, Smaller Forget-me-not (near end of bloom), Cuckooflower [Lady's Smock] (near end of bloom), Spatterdock [Yellow Pond Lily, Cow Lily], Arrowwood

Late Season: Buttercup, Common Blackberry, Larger Blue Flag Iris, Spatterdock [Yellow Pond Lily, Cow Lily], Arrowwood (near end of bloom), Bluets [Quaker Ladies, Innocence], Smaller Forget-me-not

Old Wood Road to left   *Early Season*: Buttercup, Mountain Laurel

Late Season: Buttercup, Field Hawkweed [King Devil], Mountain Laurel, Bittersweet Nightshade, Common Blackberry (near end of bloom)

Beaver Lodge Trail to left   *Early Season*: Maple-leaved Viburnum [Dockmackie] (near end of bloom), Common Blackberry (near end of bloom), Common Speedwell

Late Season: Robin's Plantain (near end of bloom), Common Cinquefoil, Buttercup, Common Blackberry (near end of bloom), Common Speedwell, Mountain Laurel, Larger Blue Flag Iris, Bittersweet Nightshade, Bluets [Quaker Ladies, Innocence]

Bluebird Trail to left (twice)   *Early Season*: No new flowers

Late Season: Smaller Forget-me-not

By exit   *Late Season*: Smooth Rose

West Mountain Road (Pleasant Valley Property)   *Early Season*: Yellow Iris

Late Season: Yellow Iris, Highbush Cranberry

Arrowhead
See Trail Information for directions to Wildflower Garden.

Wildflower Garden   *Early Season*: Day Lily (orange), Sundrops, Daisy Fleabane [Sweet Scabious], Bladder Campion, Herb Robert, Garden Lupine, Oxeye Daisy, Garden Valerian [Garden Heliotrope], Garden [European] Columbine (dark blue, pink), Multiflora Rose, Robin's Plantain, Field Hawkweed [King Devil], Common Speedwell, Canada Anemone, Rough-fruited Cinquefoil

Late Season: Garden [European] Columbine, Dame's Violet [Dame's Rocket], Rugosa Rose, White Campion, Herb Robert, Garden Lupine, Bird's-eye [Germander] Speedwell, Common Speedwell, Field Hawkweed [King Devil], Rhododendron (yellow), Multiflora Rose

Area to left of Wildflower Garden   *Early Season*: Rugosa Rose, Canada Anemone, Dame's Violet [Dame's Rocket] (near end of bloom), Cow [Tufted] Vetch

Late Season: Dame's Violet [Dame's Rocket], Rugosa Rose (many - rose colored), Wild Geranium [Spotted Cranesbill] (near end of bloom), Canada Anemone (many), Buttercup, Ground Ivy [Gill-over-the-ground], Oxeye Daisy

Near Exit   *Early Season*: Mountain Laurel (near end of bloom), Day Lily (orange)

Canoe Meadows

<u>Sacred Way Trail</u>   *See Trail Information for directions.*

Early Season: Lesser Stitchwort, Orange Hawkweed [Devil's Paintbrush], White Campion, Yarrow [Milfoil], Buttercup, Red-osier Dogwood (beginning to bloom), Cow [Tufted] Vetch, Dame's Violet [Dame's Rocket] (near end of bloom), Common Cinquefoil, Maiden Pink, Robin's Plantain (near end of bloom), Field Hawkweed [King Devil] (few), Bluets [Quaker Ladies, Innocence], Dewberry (few), Moneywort (beginning to bloom - few), Swamp Dewberry, Panicled [Gray] Dogwood, White Avens (beginning to bloom - few), Arrowwood, Meadowsweet (beginning to bloom), Bittersweet Nightshade (few), Butter-and-eggs (beginning to bloom), Multiflora Rose (few), Yellow Iris (near end of bloom), Yellow Goatsbeard

Late Season: Maiden Pink, Bluets [Quaker Ladies, Innocence], Blue-eyed Grass, Dame's Violet [Dame's Rocket], Bladder Campion, Buttercup, Larger Blue Flag Iris, Yellow Iris, Siberian Iris (purple), White Campion, Rough-fruited Cinquefoil, Daisy Fleabane [Sweet Scabious], Cow [Tufted] Vetch, Purple Loosestrife, Watercress, Orange Hawkweed [Devil's Paintbrush], Robin's Plantain, Common Cinquefoil, Yarrow [Milfoil], Field Hawkweed [King Devil], Spatterdock [Yellow Pond Lily, Cow Lily], Oxeye Daisy, Common Blackberry, Arrowwood, Blunt-leaved [Grove] Sandwort, Cuckooflower [Lady's Smock] (near end of bloom), Rough Bedstraw, Bittersweet Nightshade, Multiflora Rose, Smaller Forget-me-not, Yellow Goatsbeard, Lesser Stitchwort

Road   *See Trail Information for directions.*

Early Season: Daisy Fleabane [Sweet Scabious], Rough-fruited Cinquefoil, Hoary Alyssum (many in one place), Bladder Campion, Maiden Pink (quite a few in places), White Campion, Yarrow [Milfoil], Cow [Tufted] Vetch, Yellow Goatsbeard, Buttercup, Bittersweet Nightshade, Multiflora Rose (near end of bloom), Dame's Violet [Dame's Rocket] (near end of bloom), Canada Anemone (quite a few), White Avens, Common Cinquefoil, Silvery Cinquefoil, Panicked [Gray] Dogwood, Red-osier Dogwood (beginning to bloom), Tall Meadow Rue (beginning to bloom), Common Wood Sorrel (quite a few), Indian Cucumber Root, Common Speedwell, Poison Ivy, Lesser Stitchwort

Late Season: Daisy Fleabane [Sweet Scabious], Cow [Tufted] Vetch, Hoary Alyssum, Yarrow [Milfoil], Bladder Campion, Silvery Cinquefoil, Maiden Pink, White Campion, Field Hawkweed [King Devil], Buttercup, Aniseroot (beginning to bloom), Dame's Violet [Dame's Rocket] (near end of bloom), Multiflora Rose, Common Blackberry (near end of bloom), Orange Hawkweed [Devil's Paintbrush], Canada Anemone, White Avens, Mouse Ear, Panicled [Gray] Dogwood, Bluets [Quaker Ladies, Innocence], Wild Radish (one), Oxeye Daisy (one)

Wolf Pine Trail   *Early Season*: Some flowers listed along road plus Bluets [Quaker Ladies,, Innocence] (few), Common Blackberry (near end of bloom), Common Wood Sorrel (quite a few)

Late Season: Buttercup, Multiflora Rose, Common Speedwell, Dame's Violet [Dame's Rocket], Common

Blackberry (near end of bloom), Bluets [Quaker Ladies, Innocence], Indian Cucumber Root, Common Cinquefoil

Trails across from Hancock Shaker Village
See Trail Information for directions.

Road through field (newly mowed*) Early Season*: Yarrow [Milfoil] (many), Buttercup (few), Maiden Pink, Common St. Johnswort (beginning to bloom), Common Milkweed, Round-leaved Dogwood (few), Tall Meadow Rue (few), Meadowsweet (beginning to bloom), Daisy Fleabane [Sweet Scabious], Multiflora Rose (near end of bloom), Common Elder, Field Hawkweed [King Devil], Oxeye Daisy, Bladder Campion (few)

Late Season: Buttercup, Field Hawkweed [King Devil], Common Cinquefoil (many), Common Winter Cress [Yellow Rocket], Oxeye Daisy, Common Blackberry, Mouse Ear, Orange Hawkweed [Devil's Paintbrush], Lesser Stitchwort, Common Speedwell, Ground Ivy [Gill-over-the-ground], Yarrow [Milfoil], Field Chickweed, Blue-eyed Grass

Road to right through woods *Early Season*: Purple-flowering Raspberry (quite a few), White Avens, Shinleaf, Daisy Fleabane [Sweet Scabious], Tall Meadow Rue, Tall Nettle, Wild Leek [Ramps] (beginning to bloom)

Late Season: Ground Ivy [Gill-over-the-ground], Common Winter Cress [Yellow Rocket] (near end of bloom), Common Blackberry, Tall Meadow Rue, Golden Alexanders, Buttercup, Celandine, Canada Mayflower [Wild Lily-of-the-valley] (near end of bloom), Indian Cucumber Root, Maple-leaved Viburnum [Dockmackie], Great Angelica, Virginia Waterleaf, False Solomon's Seal [Wild Spikenard], Jack-in-the-pulpit [Indian Turnip]

Road past field toward highway *Early Season*: Some flowers listed on road through field and woods plus Common Elder, Wild Basil, Fringed Loosestrife (many)

Late Season: Ground Ivy [Gill-over-the-ground], Wood Strawberry, Tall Meadow Rue, Arrowwood (beginning to bloom), Highbush Cranberry, Buttercup, Golden Alexanders, Cinquefoil, Common Blackberry

Path partway around Shaker reservoir *Late Season*: Field Hawkweed [King Devil] (quite a few), Tall Meadow Rue (many), Orange Hawkweed [Devil's Paintbrush], Common Blackberry (many), Buttercup, Arrowwood, Highbush Cranberry, Yarrow [Milfoil] (few), Common [Philadelphia] Fleabane

FIRST TWO WEEKS IN JULY

Benedict Pond
See Trail Information for directions.

<u>Path to Pond Loop Trail (beginning at left of swimming area)</u>
Early Season: Purple-flowering Raspberry, Yarrow [Milfoil], Bladder Campion, Fringed Loosestrife, Cowwheat

Late Season: Mountain Laurel, Purple-flowering Raspberry, Buttercup, Yarrow [Milfoil], Lesser Stitchwort, Whorled [Four-leaved] Loosestrife, Field Hawkweed [King Devil], Bladder Campion, Spreading Dogbane, Shinleaf (one), Bush Honeysuckle, Oxeye Daisy

<u>Pond Loop Trail to left</u> *Early Season*: Some flowers listed on path to trail plus Indian Pipe [Corpse Plant] (many in places), Swamp Dewberry, Sweet-scented Water Lily (white - quite a few), Common Elder (near end of bloom), Tall Meadow Rue (near end of bloom), Spotted Touch-me-not [Jewelweed], Arrow-leaved Tearthumb, Swamp Candles [Yellow Loosestrife] (many in one place), Meadowsweet, Cowwheat (many in places), Whorled [Four-leaved] Loosestrife, Mountain Laurel (near end of bloom), Thimbleweed [Tall Anemone] (white and light green), White Avens, Daisy Fleabane [Sweet Scabious], Indian Cucumber Root (few)

Late Season: Whorled [Four-leaved] Loosestrife, Spreading Dogbane, Mountain Laurel (many near end of bloom), Swamp Dewberry, Wintergreen [Checkerberry], Cowwheat (many in spots), Indian Cucumber Root, Thimbleweed [Tall Anemone] (white), Spatterdock [Yellow Pond Lily, Cow Lily], Sweet-scented Water Lily (white), Tall Meadow Rue (many),

Common Elder, Indian Pipe [Corpse Plant], Purple-flowering Raspberry, Common [Philadelphia] Fleabane, White Avens, Buttercup, Cat's Ear, Bluets [Quaker Ladies, Innocence], Oxeye Daisy (few), Bladder Campion

Pleasant Valley

Path to Pike's Pond Trail including Wildflower Garden
See Trail Information for directions.

Late Season: Garden Valerian [Garden Heliotrope], Day Lily (beginning to bloom), Daisy Fleabane [Sweet Scabious], White Avens, Feverfew, Dame's Violet [Dame's Rocket], Silky Dogwood, Common Elder, Astilbe, Buttercup, Bird's-eye Primrose, Maiden Pink, Rough Cinquefoil, Oxeye Daisy, Black-eyed Susan, White Sweet Clover, Silvery Cinquefoil, Wild Radish

Pike's Pond Trail   *Early Season*: Garden Valerian [Garden Heliotrope] (quite a few), Common Milkweed, Fringed Loosestrife, Purple-flowering Raspberry, Buttercup, Enchanter's Nightshade, Purple Loosestrife, Tall Meadow Rue, Daisy Fleabane [Sweet Scabious], Black-eyed Susan, Oxeye Daisy, Bittersweet Nightshade, Common Elder, Common St. Johnswort, Dewberry, Orange Hawkweed [Devil's Paintbrush], Smaller Forget-me-not (near end of bloom)

Late Season: Swamp Dewberry, Yarrow [Milfoil], Garden Valerian [Garden Heliotrope] (quite a few), Purple-flowering Raspberry, Common Milkweed, Orange Hawkweed [Devil's Paintbrush], Field Hawkweed [King Devil], White Avens, Smaller Forget-me-not, Meadowsweet, Purple Loosestrife, Daisy Fleabane [Sweet Scabious], Small Sundrops (few), Red-berried Elder, Common Elder, Thimbleweed [Tall Anemone], Tall Meadow Rue, Common Cattail (beginning to bloom), Enchanter's Nightshade, Spreading Dogbane, Nipplewort

<u>Honeysuckle Lane</u>   *See Trail Information for directions.*

Late Season: Dame's Violet [Dame's Rocket] (near end of bloom), Common St. Johnswort, Fringed Loosestrife, Buttercup, White Avens, Garden Loosestrife, Garden Valerian [Garden Heliotrope], Purple-flowering Raspberry

<u>Path to Bluebird Trail including Wildflower Garden</u>
See Trail Information for directions.

Late Season: Garden Valerian [Garden Heliotrope], Nipplewort, Day Lily (beginning to bloom), Daisy Fleabane [Sweet Scabious], White Avens, Dame's Violet [Dame's Rocket], Common Elder, Silky Dogwood, Feverfew, Astilbe, Oxeye Daisy, Black-eyed Susan, White Sweet Clover, Maiden Pink, Silvery Cinquefoil, Cow [Tufted] Vetch, Bluets [Quaker Ladies, Innocence], Yarrow [Milfoil], Bladder Campion, White Campion

<u>Bluebird Trail</u> *Early Season*: Buttercup, Bladder Campion (few), Whorled [Four-leaved] Loosestrife

Late Season: Wild Radish, Buttercup, Orange Hawkweed [Devil's Paintbrush], Nipplewort (quite a bit in one area), Yarrow [Milfoil], Whorled [Four-leaved] Loosestrife (many), Bluets [Quaker Ladies, Innocence]

<u>Right at Yokun Trail</u> *Early Season:* Enchanter's Nightshade, Tall Meadow Rue, Meadowsweet, Daisy Fleabane [Sweet Scabious], Spatterdock [Yellow Pond Lily, Cow Lily], Purple Loosestrife

Late Season: Tall Meadow Rue, Buttercup, Orange Hawkweed [Devil's Paintbrush], Spatterdock [Yellow Pond Lily, Cow Lily], Dwarf Huckleberry, Red-osier Dogwood, Silky Dogwood, White Avens

<u>Left at Old Wood Road</u> *Early Season*: Shinleaf (few), Bittersweet Nightshade (few)

Late Season: Buttercup, Silky Dogwood, Mountain Laurel, False [White] Hellebore [Indian Poke], White Avens

<u>Left at Beaver Lodge Trail</u> *Early Season*: Purple-flowering Raspberry (few), Smaller Forget-me-not (near end of bloom), Swamp Dewberry

Late Season: Bittersweet Nightshade, Field Hawkweed [King Devil] (one), Buttercup, White Avens, Dwarf Huckleberry, Dewberry (one), Mountain Laurel (near end of bloom)

<u>Left at Bluebird Trail</u> (twice) *Early and Late Seasons*: No new flowers were observed.

Arrowhead
See Trail Information for directions to Wildflower Garden.

<u>Wildflower Garden</u>   *Early Season*: Garden Valerian [Garden Heliotrope] (white and pink), Sundrops, Black-eyed Susan, Daisy Fleabane [Sweet Scabious], Fringed Loosestrife, Black Snakeroot [Black Cohosh] (many), Bladder Campion, Creeping Bellflower, Hydrangea, Oxeye Daisy, Astilbe, Rugosa Rose, Day Lily (orange)

Late Season: Hydrangea, Bladder Campion, Herb Robert, Black-eyed Susan, Daisy Fleabane [Sweet Scabious], Rugosa Rose, Cow [Tufted] Vetch, Day Lily, Garden Valerian [Garden Heliotrope] (white, light orchid), Astilbe (white), Garden Loosestrife, Sundrops, Black Snakeroot [Black Cohosh] (beginning to bloom)

<u>Area to left of Wildflower Garden</u>   *Early Season*: Canada Anemone, Musk Mallow, Hedge Bindweed, Cow [Tufted] Vetch, Rough-fruited [Sulphur] Cinquefoil, Common Milkweed

Late Season: Day Lily, Rugosa Rose, Musk Mallow, Canada Anemone, Daisy Fleabane [Sweet Scabious], Garden Valerian [Garden Heliotrope], Cow [Tufted] Vetch, Common Milkweed (beginning to bloom)

Canoe Meadows

<u>Sacred Way Trail</u>   *See Trail Information for Directions.*

Early Season: Common Milkweed (many in places), Cow [Tufted] Vetch, Yarrow [Milfoil], Daisy Fleabane [Sweet Scabious], Meadowsweet (many), Buttercup, Bladder Campion, Agrimony, Purple Loosestrife, Watercress, Spotted Touch-me-not [Jewelweed], Swamp Milkweed (beginning to bloom), Tall Nettle, Red-osier Dogwood, Fringed Loosestrife (many), Canada Lily [Meadow Lily, Wild Yellow Lily], Maiden Pink, Common St. Johnswort, Round-leaved Dogwood, Spatterdock [Yellow Pond Lily, Cow Lily], Swamp Dewberry, Shinleaf, Wild Leek [Ramps], Bluets [Quaker Ladies, Innocence], Swamp Candles [Yellow Loosestrife] (many in one place), Bittersweet Nightshade, Canada Thistle, Blue Vervain, Common Elder (many in one place)

Late Season: Common Milkweed, Common Cinquefoil, Purple Loosestrife, Common Arrowhead, Canada Lily [Meadow Lily, Wild Yellow Lily], Maiden Pink, Common St. Johnswort, Buttercup, Red-berried Elder, Blue Vervain, Northern Bugleweed, Tall Meadow Rue, Dame's Violet [Dame's Rocket], Camphorweed, Meadowsweet, Motherwort, White Campion, White Avens, Cow [Tufted] Vetch, Silvery Cinquefoil, Yellow Iris, Daisy Fleabane [Sweet Scabious], Red-osier Dogwood, Fringed Loosestrife, Yellow Goatsbeard, Yarrow [Milfoil], Swamp Dewberry, Swamp Candles [Yellow Loosestrife], Bittersweet Nightshade, Common Elder, Watercress, Common Evening Primrose, Hedge Bindweed, Swamp Milkweed (beginning to bloom), Butter-and-eggs

Road   *See Trail Information for directions.*

Early Season: (field mowed) Common Milkweed, Yarrow [Milfoil], Hoary Alyssum, Bladder Campion, Butter-and-eggs, Spotted Touch-me-not [Jewelweed], Pale Dogwood, White Avens, Agrimony, White Campion, Buttercup, Fringed Loosestrife, Enchanter's Nightshade, Wild Hydrangea, Maiden Pink, Purple Loosestrife, Meadowsweet, Red-osier Dogwood, Common Cattail, Bittersweet Nightshade, Tall Meadow Rue, Swamp Dewberry, Daisy Fleabane [Sweet Scabious], Cow [Tufted] Vetch

Late Season: Common Milkweed, Hedge Bindweed, Motherwort, Tall Meadow Rue, Dame's Violet [Dame's Rocket], Fringed Loosestrife, Day Lily, White Campion, Sweet Viburnum [Nannyberry], Daisy Fleabane [Sweet Scabious] (many in spots), White Avens, Hoary Alyssum, Aniseroot (near end of bloom), Enchanter's Nightshade, Meadowsweet (beginning to bloom), Common Elder, Spotted Touch-me-not [Jewelweed] (beginning to bloom), Canada Anemone (near end of bloom), Privet, Rough-fruited [Sulphur] Cinquefoil, Lesser Stitchwort, Bladder Campion, Cow [Tufted] Vetch, Yarrow [Milfoil], Alfalfa [Lucerne], White Avens, Buttercup, Common [Philadelphia] Fleabane, Wild Basil, Maiden Pink, Orange Hawkweed [Devil's Paintbrush], Silky Dogwood, Shinleaf (one), Multiflora Rose (near end of bloom)

Wolf Pine Trail   *Early Season*: Swamp Dewberry, Wild Hydrangea, Daisy Fleabane [Sweet Scabious], Indian Pipe [Corpse Plant] (many in one place), One-flowered Cancerroot [Ghost Pipe], White Avens

Late Season: Buttercup, Silky Dogwood, Dewberry, Tall Meadow Rue, Common Cinquefoil, Dame's Violet [Dame's Rocket], Wintergreen [Checkerberry], White Campion, Maiden Pink

Trails across from Hancock Shaker Village
See Trail Information for directions.

Road through field *Early Season*: Maiden Pink, Black-eyed Susan, Daisy Fleabane [Sweet Scabious], Oxeye Daisy, Yarrow [Milfoil] (quite a few), Common St. Johnswort, Wild Radish, Common Milkweed (many in spots), Meadowsweet, Field Hawkweed [King Devil] (few), Orange Hawkweed [Devil's Paintbrush] (few)

Late Season: Maiden Pink, Oxeye Daisy, Daisy Fleabane [Sweet Scabious], Yarrow [Milfoil], Tall Meadow Rue, Red-osier Dogwood, Multiflora Rose (near end of bloom), Buttercup, Field Hawkweed [King Devil], Orange Hawkweed [Devil's Paintbrush], Rough-fruited [Sulphur] Cinquefoil, Silky Dogwood, Rough Cinquefoil, Lesser Stitchwort, Wild Parsnip, Common Milkweed (beginning to bloom), Common Elder, Common St. Johnswort, Meadowsweet (beginning to bloom), Black-eyed Susan, Common Cinquefoil, Common Evening Primrose, Bladder Campion, Purple-flowering Raspberry

Road to right through woods *Early Season*: White Avens, Fringed Loosestrife (many in spots), Purple-flowering Raspberry (many in spots), Spotted Touch-me-not [Jewelweed], Celandine (near end of bloom), Great Angelica, Common Elder, Enchanter's Nightshade, Shinleaf, Agrimony, Wild Leek [Ramps] , Tall Meadow Rue (near end of bloom)

Late Season: Purple-flowering Raspberry, White Avens, Common Blackberry (near end of bloom), Rough Cinquefoil, Great Angelica, Spotted Touch-me-not [Jewelweed] (beginning to bloom), Daisy Fleabane [Sweet Scabious], Tall Meadow Rue, Buttercup

<u>Road past field toward highway</u> *Late Season:* White Avens, Tall Meadow Rue, Small Bedstraw, Buttercup

<u>Path partway around Shaker reservoir</u> *Late Season:* Tall Meadow Rue (many in spots), Common Elder, Silky Dogwood, Daisy Fleabane [Sweet Scabious], Oxeye Daisy, Blue-eyed Grass, Orange Hawkweed [Devil's Paintbrush] (few), Black-eyed Susan

<u>Road to highway continued</u> *Late Season:* Buttercup, Orange Hawkweed [Devil's Paintbrush], White Avens (quite a few), Common Cinquefoil, Small Bedstraw

LAST TWO WEEKS IN JULY

Benedict Pond
See Trail Information for directions.

<u>Path to Pond Loop Trail (beginning at left of swimming area)</u>
Early Season: Meadowsweet, Spreading Dogbane, Common St. Johnswort, Yarrow [Milfoil], Cowwheat, Bladder Campion, Oxeye Daisy, Purple-flowering Raspberry, Buttercup

Late Season: Yarrow [Milfoil], Purple-flowering Raspberry, Buttercup, Spreading Dogbane, Whorled [Four-leaved] Loosestrife

<u>Pond Loop Trail to left</u> *Early Season*: Some flowers listed on <u>Path to Pond Loop Trail</u> plus Sharp-leaved [Mountain, Whorled] Aster (beginning to bloom), Wintergreen [Checkerberry] (many), Goldenrod (beginning to bloom), Indian Hemp, Indian Pipe [Corpse Plant] (many in spots), Panicled Hawkweed, Sweet-scented Water Lily (white), Spotted Touch-me-not [Jewelweed], Arrow-leaved Tearthumb, Swamp Candles [Yellow Loosestrife], Common Arrowhead, Flat-topped Aster (beginning to bloom), Cowwheat, Common Elder (near end of bloom), Spotted St. Johnswort, Spatterdock [Yellow Pond Lily, Cow Lily], Common Cattail, Horse Balm [Richweed, Stoneroot], Tall Meadow Rue, Pointed-leaved Tick Trefoil (few), White Avens, Enchanter's Nightshade, Helleborine, Fringed Loosestrife, Daisy Fleabane [Sweet Scabious], Agrimony, Spotted Joe-Pye Weed, Tall Rattlesnake Root [Gall-of-the-earth]

Late Season: Spreading Dogbane, Bladder Campion, Sweet-scented Water Lily (white), Shinleaf, Spatterdock [Yellow Pond Lily, Cow Lily], Common Elder, Tall Meadow Rue, Spotted Touch-me-not [Jewelweed] (beginning to bloom), Swamp Candles [Yellow Loosestrife] (many), Marsh Skullcap, Dwarf Huckleberry, Daisy Fleabane [Sweet Scabious], Meadowsweet, Sweet Viburnum [Nannyberry], Cowwheat (many), Enchanter's Nightshade, Indian Pipe [Corpse Plant], Thimbleweed [Tall Anemone], Fringed Loosestrife, Purple-flowering Raspberry, Buttercup, Whorled [Four-leaved] Loosestrife (near end of bloom), Yarrow [Milfoil]

Pleasant Valley

Path to Pike's Pond Trail including wildflower garden
See Trail Information for directions.

Late Season: Feverfew, Fringed Loosestrife, Silky Dogwood (near end of bloom), Astilbe, Oswego Tea [Bee Balm], Day Lily (orange), Common Mullein, Wild Radish, Meadowsweet

Pike's Pond Trail   *Early Season*: Garden Valerian [Garden Heliotrope], Meadowsweet, Maiden Pink, Common St. Johnswort, Wild Bergamot, Spotted Joe-Pye Weed (beginning to bloom), Virgin's Bower (beginning to bloom- many), Purple-flowering Raspberry, Enchanter's Nightshade, Purple Loosestrife, Daisy Fleabane [Sweet Scabious], Agrimony, Buttercup, Black-eyed Susan (few), Fringed Loosestrife, Marsh St. Johnswort, Marsh Skullcap, Mad-dog Skullcap, Helleborine, Common Cattail, Boneset [Thoroughwort], Swamp Milkweed, Large-leaved Aster, Horse Balm [Richweed, Stoneroot], Indian Pipe [Corpse Plant], Wild Basil, Smaller Forget-me-not, Buttonbush

Late Season: Meadowsweet, Yarrow [Milfoil], Garden Valerian [Garden Heliotrope] (light lilac and white), Common St. Johnswort, Daisy Fleabane [Sweet Scabious], Common Milkweed, Fringed Loosestrife, Purple-Flowering Raspberry, Tall Meadow Rue, Common Arrowhead, Wild Bergamot. Enchanter's Nightshade, Purple Loosestrife, Smaller Forget-me-not, Buttercup, Agrimony, Black-eyed Susan, Common Cattail, Swamp Milkweed

Honeysuckle Lane *See Trail Information for directions.*

Early Season: Garden Loosestrife, Spotted Touch-me-not [Jewelweed], Dame's Violet [Dame's Rocket]

Late Season: Common St. Johnswort, Garden Valerian [Garden Heliotrope], Fringed Loosestrife, Garden Loosestrife, Meadowsweet, Common Milkweed, Yellow Avens, Purple-flowering Raspberry, Agrimony

Path to Bluebird Trail *See Trail Information for directions.*

Early Season: Meadowsweet, Bladder Campion

Path to Bluebird Trail including wildflower garden
Late Season: Feverfew, Silky Dogwood (near end of bloom), Buttercup, Astilbe, Oswego Tea [Bee Balm], Day Lily (orange), Motherwort, Common Mullein, Wild Radish, Bladder Campion (few), Oxeye Daisy (few), Common Milkweed (near end of bloom), Black-eyed Susan, Yellow Goatsbeard, Yarrow [Milfoil], Hedge Bindweed

Bluebird Trail *Early Season*: Yarrow [Milfoil], Black-eyed Susan, Meadowsweet, Goldenrod, Spiked Lobelia (one), Common St. Johnswort

Late Season: Lady's Thumb, Common St. Johnswort, Meadowsweet, Whorled [Four-leaved] Loosestrife (near end of bloom), Yarrow [Milfoil]

<u>Yokun Trail to right</u>   *Early Season*: Helleborine, Meadowsweet, Purple Loosestrife, Cattail, Daisy Fleabane [Sweet Scabious], Pale Dogwood, Spotted Joe-Pye Weed

Late Season: Tall Meadow Rue (one), Indian Pipe [Corpse Plant] (one), Meadowsweet, Lesser Daisy Fleabane, Spatterdock [Yellow Pond Lily, Cow Lily], Steeplebush [Hardhack], Purple Loosestrife, Agrimony, White Avens, Fringed Loosestrife

<u>Old Wood Road to left</u> *Early Season*: Common Arrowhead, Spotted St. Johnswort, Agrimony, Purple-flowering Raspberry

Late Season: Buttercup, Meadowsweet, Purple Loosestrife, Spotted St. Johnswort, Bittersweet Nightshade

<u>Beaver Lodge Trail to left</u>   *Early Season*: Enchanter's Nightshade, Buttercup, Swamp Milkweed

Late Season: Agrimony, Enchanter's Nightshade, Buttercup, White Avens, Meadowsweet, Purple Loosestrife, Virgin's Bower, Spatterdock [Yellow Pond Lily, Cow Lily] (few), Dewberry (few)

<u>Bluebird Trail to left (twice</u>)   *Early Season*: Indian Pipe [Corpse Plant] (one)

Late Season: Lady's Thumb

Irregular Flowers

Often no apparent leaves at time of bloom

1A Skunk Cabbage (x 1/4)

Basal leaves only

1B Jack-in-the-pulpit (x 2/3)
[Indian Turnip]
(also green and white)

1C Pink Lady's Slipper (x 1/2)
[Moccasin Flower]

1D Shooting Star (x 1/2)

Alternate Leaves

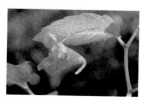

1E Spotted Touch-me-not (x 1/2)
[Jewelweed]

1F Wood Betony (x 1/2)
[Lousewort]

Irregular Flowers

Alternate Leaves

2A Butter-and-eggs (x 1/2)

2B Wild Monkshood (x 1/2)

2C Alfalfa (x 1/2)
[Lucerne]

2D Larger Yellow Lady's Slipper
(x 1/2)

2E Spiked Lobelia (x 1)

2F Helleborine (x 1/2)

Irregular Flowers

Alternate Leaves

3A Great Lobelia (x 1/2)

Opposite Leaves

3B Turtlehead (x 1/2)

3D Pink Turtlehead (x 1/2)

3C Horse Balm
[Richweed or Stoneroot](x 3/4)

3E Bird's-eye [Germander]
Speedwell (x 1/2)

3F Ground Ivy (x 1/2)
[Gill-over-the-ground]

Irregular Flowers or Flower with Two Regular Parts

Opposite Leaves

4A Wild Bergamot
(x 1/2)

4B Common Speedwell
(x 3/4)

4C Motherwort
(x 1/2)

4D Selfheal (x 3/4)
[Heal-all]

4E Cowwheat (x 1/2)

4F Wild Basil (x 1/2)
(pink or lilac)

Vines

4G Cow [Tufted] Vetch (x 1/2)

4H Hog Peanut
(x 1/2)

Flower With Two Regular Parts

4I Enchanter's
Nightshade (x 1/2)

Flowers with Three Regular Parts

Basal Leaves

5A Wild Ginger (x 1/2)

5B Common Arrowhead (x 1/2)

Alternate Leaves

5C Yellow Iris (x 1/4)

5D Crested Iris (x 1/2)

Whorled Leaves

5F Large-flowered Trillium (x 1/3)
(flower white turning pink)

5E Larger Blue Flag Iris (x 1/4)

Flowers with Three or Four Regular Parts

Three Regular Parts - Whorled Leaves

6B Wake-robin (x 2/5)
[Birthroot, Purple or Red Trillium]

6A Painted Trillium (x 2/5)

6C Toad Trillium (x 2/5)
[Toadshade]

Four Regular Parts - Alternate Leaves

6D Dame's Violet (x 1/2)
[Dame's Rocket]
(pink, purple, or white)

6G Cuckooflower (x 1/2)
[Lady's Smock]
(also pink)

6E Tall Meadow Rue (x 1/2)   6F Wild Radish (x 1)

Flowers with Four Regular Parts

Alternate Leaves

7A Garlic Mustard
(x 7/8)

7B Hoary Alyssum
(x 1)

7C Canada Mayflower (x 1/2)
[Wild Lily-of-the-valley]

7D Common Evening Primrose (x 1/2)

Whorled Leaves

7E Bunchberry (x 1/2)
[Dwarf Cornel]

Opposite or Whorled Leaves

7F Toothwort (x 1/2)
[Crinkleroot]

7G Bluets (x 2/3)
[Quaker Ladies, Innocence]

Flowers with Four or Five Regular Parts

Shrubs

8A Silky Dogwood (x 1/2)

8B Panicled [Gray] Dogwood (x 1/2)

8C Buttonbush (x 1/2)

Vine

8D Virgin's Bower (x 2/3)

Five Regular Parts

No Apparent Leaves at Flowering Time

Basal Leaves Only

8F Wild Sarsaparilla (x 1/2)

8E Indian Pipe [Corpse Plant] (x 2/3)

Flowers with Five Regular Parts

Basal Leaves Only

9A Spatterdock (x 1/4)
[Yellow Pond Lily, Cow Lily]

9B Common Wood Sorrel
(x 2/3)

9C Foamflower (x 1/2)
[False Miterwort]

Alternate Leaves

9D Wild Carrot (x 2/5)
[Queen Anne's Lace, Bird's Nest]

9E Yarrow [Milfoil] (x 2/5)

9F Yellow Wood Sorrel
(x 1/2)

9G Rough-fruited
[Sulphur] Cinquefoil (x 1)

9H Silvery Cinquefoil
(x 1)

9I Common Cinquefoil (x 1)

Flowers with Five Regular Parts

Alternate Leaves

10A Spotted Knapweed
(x 1/2) (pink, purple,
or white)

10B Trailing Arbutus
[Mayflower] (x 1)
(pink or white)

10C Common Blackberry
(x 1/2)

10D Wintergreen
[Checkerberry]
(x 1)

10E Common Mullein (x 1/2)

10F Smaller
Forget-me-not
(x 1)

10G Agrimony (x 1/2)

10H Musk Mallow (x 1/2)

10I Yellow Avens
(x 1)

Flowers with Five Regular Parts

Alternate Leaves

11A Marsh Marigold
[Cowslip] (x 1/2)

Opposite or Whorled Leaves

11B Wild Geranium
[Spotted Cranesbill] (x 1/2)

11C Swamp Milkweed (x 2/3)
(pink to rose-purple)

11D Swamp Candles
[Yellow Loosestrife] (x 1/2)

11E Canada Anemone (x 2/3)

11F Whorled [Four-leaved]
Loosestrife (x 2/3)

Flowers with Five Regular Parts

Opposite or Whorled Leaves

12A Herb Robert
(x 3/4)

12B Garden Valerian
[Garden Heliotrope] (x 1/2)

Opposite Leaves

12C Spotted St. Johnswort
(x 1)

12D Closed [Bottle] Gentian (x 1/2)

12E Ragged Robin
[Cuckooflower] (x 1/2)

12F Carolina Spring Beauty
(x 2/3)

12G Maiden Pink
(x 2/3)

12H White Campion
(x 1/2)

12I Bladder Campion
(x 1/2)

12J Common
St. Johnswort (x 1/2)

Flowers with Five Regular Parts

Opposite Leaves

13A Spreading Dogbane (x 1)

13B Blue Vervain (x 2/3)

13C Bouncing Bet [Soapwort]
(x 1/2) (pink or white)

Shrubs

13E Hawthorn (x 1/2)

13D Common or Smooth Shadbush (x 1/2)

13F Common Elder (x 1/2)

13G Wild Hydrangea (x 1/3)

Flowers with Five Regular Parts

Shrubs

14A Pink Azalea [Pinxter Flower] (x 1/2)

14B Steeplebush [Hardhack] (x 1/3)

14C Morrow's Honeysuckle
(x 1/2)

14D Hybrid of Morrow's and
Tartarian Honeysuckle (x 1/2)

14E Multiflora Rose (x 1/2)

14F Meadowsweet (x 1)

Flowers with Five Regular Parts

Shrubs

15A Rugosa Rose (x 1/2)

15B Purple-flowering Raspberry
(x 1/2)

15C Maple-leaved Viburnum
[Dockmackie] (x 1/2)

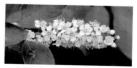

15D Chokecherry (x 1/2)

15E Mountain Laurel(x 1/2)

Flowers with Five or Six Regular Parts

Five Regular Parts - Shrubs

16A Highbush Cranberry (x 1/2)
(leaves shaped like Maple leaves)

16B Hobblebush (x 1/2)

Five Regular Parts - Vines

16C Hedge Bindweed (x 1/2)

16D Dewberry (x 1/2)

Six Regular Parts - Vine

16E Bittersweet Nightshade (x 1/2)

16F Wild Balsam Apple
[Wild Cucumber] (x 1/4)

Flowers with Six Regular Parts

Basal Leaves Only

17A Trout Lily
[Yellow Adder's Tongue] (x 1/2)

17B Yellow Clintonia
[Bluebead] (x 1/2)

17C Blue-eyed Grass (x 1/2)

17D Siberian Scilla
[Spring Squill] (x 1/2)

Alternate Leaves

17E Hairy Solomon's Seal (x 1/2)

17F Great Solomon's Seal (x 1/2)

Flowers with Six Regular Parts

Alternate Leaves

18A False [White] Hellibore
[Indian Poke] (x 1/2)

18B Sessile-leaved Bellwort
[Wild Oats] (x 1/2)

18C False Solomon's Seal [Wild Spikenard] (x 1/2)

Opposite or Whorled Leaves

18D Mayapple [Mandrake]
(x 1/2)

18E Indian Cucumber Root
(x 1/2)

Flowers with Six or Seven Regular Parts

Opposite or Whorled Leaves

19B Turk's-cap Lily (x 1/2)

19A Purple Loosestrife (x 1/2)

Seven or More Regular Parts
Basal Leaves

19C Canada Lily
[Meadow Lily, Wild Yellow Lily]
(x 1/2) (yellow, orange, or red)

19D Bloodroot (x 1/2)

Flowers with Seven or More Regular Parts

Basal Leaves

20A Sweet-scented Water Lily (x 1/2)

20B Field Hawkweed [King Devil] (x 1/2)

20C Orange Hawkweed [Devil's Paintbrush] (x 1/2)

Alternate Leaves

20E Black-eyed Susan (x 1/2)

20D Golden or Round-leaved Ragwort (x 1/2)

20F Yellow Goatsbeard (x 1/2)

20G Nipplewort (x 1/2)

Flowers with Seven or More Regular Parts

Alternate Leaves

21A Robin's Plantain (x 1/2)

21B Common [Philadelphia]
Fleabane (x 1/2)
(has clasping leaves)

21C Tall [Green-headed] Coneflower (x 1/2)

21D Daisy Fleabane
[Sweet Scabious] (x 1/2)

Opposite or Whorled Leaves

21E Starflower (x 1)

Seven or More Regular Parts or Parts Indistinguishable

Seven or More Regular Parts

Opposite or Whorled Leaves

22A Cup Plant [Indian Cup] (x 1/3)

Opposite Leaves

22B Showy Sunflower
(x 1/2)

Parts Indistinguishable - Alternate Leaves

22C Bull Thistle (x 1/2)

22D Canada Thistle (x 1/2)

22E Common Burdock (x 1/2)

22F Golden Alexanders (x 1/2)

Flowers with Parts Indistinguishable

Alternate Leaves

23A White Baneberry
[Doll's Eyes] (x 1/2)

23C Black Snakeroot
[Black Cohosh] (x 1/2)

Opposite or Whorled Leaves

23B White Snakeroot (x 1/2)

23D Boneset [Thoroughwort] (x 1/2) (leaves lanced-shaped and have no
stem but attach directly to main stem)

Flowers with Parts Indistinguishable

Opposite or Whorled Leaves

24A Spotted Joe-Pye Weed (x 1/2)

Opposite Leaves

24B Tall Nettle
(x 1/2)

Goldenrods

24C Blue-stemmed [Wreath] Goldenrod (x 1/2)

24E Silverrod (x 1/2)

24D Zigzag [Broad-leaved] Goldenrod (x 1/2)

Asters

Heart-shaped Leaves
Basal Leaves Less than 3 Inches Wide or None

25A Heart-leaved Aster
(x 2/5) (light blue-violet,
light rose, or white)

25B White Wood Aster (x 2/5)

Basal Leaves 3 in. Wide or More

25C Lowrie's Aster (x 2/5)
(stem to leaf is winged;
flowers pale blue, blue, or
pinkish)

25D Large-leaved Aster (x 2/5)
(violet or lavender)

25E Schreber's Aster (x 2/5)

Asters

Leaves not Heart-shaped

26A Sharp-leaved [Mountain or Whorled] Aster (x 2/5)
(upper leaves are larger than lower leaves and appear to be whorled;
flowers white or purple tinged)

26B Calico [Starved] Aster (x 1/2)
(flowers white or purple tinged,
have 9-15 petals and often have
some purple disks)

26C Panicled Aster (x 1/2)
(leaves narrowly lance-shaped;
flower heads 0.75-1 in. wide;
white or tinged with violet)

26D New England Aster (x 1/2)
(stem hairy; leaves lance-shaped, clasping; flower 1-2 in.;
violet-purple, occasionally rose-colored or white)

Aster

Leaves not Heart-shaped

27A Flat-topped Aster (x 2/5)
(flowers 0.5-0.75 in. wide and arranged in fairly flat clusters)

27B Purple-stemmed Aster (x 2/5)
(stem hairy and sometimes purple; clasping leaves; flowers 1-1.5 in. wide;
plant 2-8 ft. high; center sometimes yellow and sometimes reddish brown)

Arrowhead
See Trail Information for directions to Wildflower Garden.

<u>Wildflower Garden</u>   *Early Season*: Black Snakeroot [Black Cohosh], Garden Valerian [Garden Heliotrope], Day Lily (yellow), Daisy Fleabane [Sweet Scabious], Day Lily (orange), Cow [Tufted] Vetch, Fringed Loosestrife, Turk's-cap Lily, Creeping Bellflower, Black-eyed Susan, Bladder Campion

Late Season: Hydrangea, Daisy Fleabane [Sweet Scabious], Garden Valerian [Garden Heliotrope] (lilac and white), Black-eyed Susan, Black Snakeroot [Black Cohosh], Fringed Loosestrife, Day Lily (orange), Creeping Bellflower

<u>Area to left of Wildflower Garden</u>   *Early Season*: Hedge Bindweed, Musk Mallow, Black-eyed Susan, Wild Carrot [Queen Anne's Lace, Bird's Nest]

Late Season: Day Lily (orange), Hedge Bindweed, Musk Mallow, Black-eyed Susan, Wild Carrot [Queen Anne's Lace, Bird's Nest], Common Milkweed, Daisy Fleabane [Sweet Scabious], Oxeye Daisy

Canoe Meadows

<u>Sacred Way Trail</u>   *See Trail Information for directions.*

Early Season: Lesser Stitchwort, Yarrow [Milfoil] (quite a few), Daisy Fleabane [Sweet Scabious], Goldenrod (beginning to bloom), Cow [Tufted] Vetch, Meadowsweet (many), Common Milkweed (near end of bloom- many in spots), Common Evening Primrose (few), Buttercup (few), Fringed Loosestrife, Purple Loosestrife (many), Spotted Joe-Pye Weed (many), Common Arrowhead, Blue Vervain (quite a few), Spotted Touch-me-not [Jewelweed] (beginning to bloom), Swamp Milkweed (beginning to bloom), Hedge Bindweed (beginning to bloom), Common Milkweed (near end of bloom-many in spots), Maiden Pink, Common St. Johnswort (near end of bloom), Bluets [Quaker Ladies, Innocence] (few), Steeplebush [Hardhack] (few), Oxeye Daisy (near end of bloom- few)

Late Season: Meadowsweet, Yarrow [Milfoil] (near end of bloom), Cow [Tufted] Vetch, Goldenrod (beginning to bloom), Spotted Touch-me-not [Jewelweed], Common Milkweed, Yellow Goatsbeard (one), Hedge Bindweed (many), Blue Vervain, Daisy Fleabane [Sweet Scabious] (few), Canada Lily [Meadow Lily, Wild Yellow Lily] (few), Bluets [Quaker Ladies, Innocence] (few), Black-eyed Susan (few), Silky Dogwood (near end of bloom), Butter-and-eggs, Canada Thistle, Agrimony (few), Common Evening Primrose, Purple Loosestrife, Swamp Milkweed, Common St. Johnswort, Fringed Loosestrife (quite a few), Maiden Pink, Buttercup, Swamp Candles [Yellow Loosestrife], Day Lily (orange)

Road: *See Trail Information for directions.*

Early Season: Daisy Fleabane [Sweet Scabious], Hoary Alyssum, Bladder Campion, Silvery Cinquefoil, Butter-and-eggs, Alfalfa [Lucerne], Common Burdock, Bouncing Bet [Soapwort], Motherwort, Wild Balsam Apple [Wild Cucumber], White Campion, Helleborine, Fringed Loosestrife, Tall Nettle, Spotted Touch-me-not [Jewelweed], Enchanter's Nightshade, Wild Basil, Agrimony, Cup Plant [Indian Cup], Maiden Pink, Rough-fruited Cinquefoil, Yarrow [Milfoil], Flat-topped Aster, Buttercup, Purple Loosestrife, Pale Dogwood, Common Cattail, Meadowsweet, Fringed

Loosestrife, Sharp-leaved [Mountain, Whorled] Aster, Tall Meadow Rue, Indian Pipe [Corpse Plant], Spotted Joe-Pye Weed, Goldenrod (beginning to bloom), White Wood Aster, Black-eyed Susan (near end of bloom- few)

Late Season: Daisy Fleabane [Sweet Scabious], Maiden Pink, Hoary Alyssum, Bladder Campion, White Campion, Common Mullein (beginning to bloom), Alfalfa [Lucerne], Yarrow [Milfoil], Agrimony, Bouncing Bet [Soapwort], Enchanter's Nightshade, White Avens, Tall Meadow Rue, Buttercup, Wild Hydrangea, Day Lily, Tall Nettle, Wild Radish, Dame's Violet [Dame's Rocket] (near end of bloom), Cup Plant [Indian Cup], Pokeweed, Wild Balsam Apple [Wild Cucumber] (beginning to bloom), Wild Carrot [Queen Anne's Lace, Bird's Nest], Fringed Loosestrife, Cow [Tufted] Vetch, Spotted Touch-me-not [Jewelweed]. Aniseroot (near end of bloom), Goldenrod (beginning to bloom), Purple Loosestrife, Meadowsweet, Common Cattail, White Sweet Clover, Common St. Johnswort, Silky Dogwood (near end of bloom)

<u>Wolf Pine Trail</u>   *Early Season*: Agrimony, Spotted Touch-me-not [Jewelweed], Indian Pipe [Corpse Plant], Wild Hydrangea, Daisy Fleabane [Sweet Scabious], Helleborine

Late Season: Agrimony, Buttercup, Bittersweet Nightshade, Dewberry (one), Enchanter's Nightshade, Common Milkweed (near end of bloom), Dame's Violet [Dame's Rocket] (near end of bloom), Indian Pipe [Corpse Plant], Pinesap [False Beechdrops] (beginning to bloom), White Avens, Daisy Fleabane [Sweet Scabious], White Campion

Trails across from Hancock Shaker Village
See Trail Information for directions.

Road through field   *Early Season:* Common St. Johnswort (quite a few), Yarrow [Milfoil] (many), Maiden Pink, Black-eyed Susan (few), Oxeye Daisy (few), Wild Radish (few), Daisy Fleabane [Sweet Scabious], Wild Carrot [Queen Anne's Lace, Bird's Nest], Swamp Milkweed (quite a few), Common Evening Primrose (beginning to bloom), Rough Cinquefoil, Spotted Touch-me-not [Jewelweed] (beginning to bloom), Meadowsweet (many), Orange Hawkweed [Devil's Paintbrush] (few), Goldenrod (beginning to bloom), Common Milkweed (many in places), Agrimony, Blue Vervain (beginning to bloom), Bladder Campion, Spotted Knapweed (beginning to bloom), Narrow-leaved Mountain Mint, Narrow-leaved Meadowsweet, Thimbleweed [Tall Anemone], Common Mullein, Enchanter's Nightshade, Nipplewort, Centaury

Late Season: Maiden Pink, Meadowsweet (beginning to bloom), Yarrow [Milfoil], Common St. Johnswort, Silvery Cinquefoil, Rough-fruited Cinquefoil, Bladder Campion (near end of bloom), Buttercup, Rough Cinquefoil, Black-eyed Susan, Blue-eyed Grass, Garden Valerian [Garden Heliotrope], Orange Hawkweed [Devil's Paintbrush], Common Milkweed (many), Goldenrod (beginning to bloom), Daisy Fleabane [Sweet Scabious] (many), Oxeye Daisy (many in spots), Wild Carrot [Queen Anne's Lace, Bird's Nest], Spotted Joe-Pye Weed (beginning to bloom), Common Mullein, Common Evening Primrose.

Road to right through woods   *Early Season*: Wild Basil, Daisy Fleabane [Sweet Scabious], Enchanter's Nightshade, Fringed Loosestrife, Purple-flowering Raspberry (quite a few), Helleborine, White Avens (beginning to bloom), Spikenard, Spotted Touch-me-not [Jewelweed] (beginning to bloom), Tall Nettle, Sharp-leaved [Mountain., Whorled] Aster, Indian Pipe [Corpse Plant] (many in one area), Pointed-leaved Tick Trefoil

Late Season: Spotted Touch-me-not [Jewelweed] (beginning to bloom), Enchanter's Nightshade, Common Milkweed, Daisy Fleabane [Sweet Scabious], Tall Meadow Rue (near end of bloom), Fringed Loosestrife, Agrimony, Purple-flowering Raspberry, Wild Basil, Common Elder, White Avens (near end of bloom), Tall Nettle, Yarrow [Milfoil]

Road past field toward highway   *Early Season*: Daisy Fleabane [Sweet Scabious], Spotted Touch-me-not [Jewelweed] (beginning to bloom), Meadowsweet, Buttercup, Common St. Johnswort, Fringed Loosestrife, Wild Carrot [Queen Anne's Lace, Bird's Nest]

Late Season: Common Milkweed, White Avens (near end of bloom), Daisy Fleabane [Sweet Scabious], Common Elder, Buttercup, Round-leaved Dogwood, Oxeye Daisy, Common St. Johnswort, White Sweet Clover

Path partway around Shaker reservoir   *Early Season*: Meadowsweet (many), Yarrow [Milfoil], Goldenrod, Spotted St. Johnswort, Common St. Johnswort, Black-eyed Susan, Steeplebush [Hardhack] (beginning to bloom), Wild Carrot [Queen Anne's Lace, Bird's Nest]

Late Season: Yarrow [Milfoil], Common Blackberry, Orange Hawkweed [Devil's Paintbrush], Blue-eyed Grass, Tall Meadow Rue, Dewberry, Common Elder, Meadowsweet, Oxeye Daisy, Common St. Johnswort, Black-eyed Susan, Pale Dogwood, Common Mullein (beginning to bloom), Common Milkweed, Bittersweet Nightshade (few), Agrimony

Road to highway continued   *Late Season:* Common Elder, Fringed Loosestrife (many in two places), Common Cattail, Narrow-leaved Cattail, Enchanter's Nightshade, Black-eyed Susan, Maiden Pink

FIRST TWO WEEKS IN AUGUST

Benedict Pond
See Trail Information for directions.

<u>Path to Pond Loop Trail (beginning at left of swimming area</u>)
Early Season: White Wood Aster

Late Season: Meadowsweet, Purple-flowering Raspberry, Spreading Dogbane, Common St. Johnswort, Goldenrod, Yarrow [Milfoil], Bladder Campion, White Wood Aster

<u>Pond Loop Trail to left</u>   *Early Season*: Silverrod, Spotted Touch-me-not [Jewelweed], Sharp-leaved [Mountain, Whorled] Aster (many in spots), White Wood Aster, Boneset [Thoroughwort], Panicled Hawkweed, Sweet-scented Water Lily (white), Meadowsweet (near end of bloom), Purple-stemmed Aster, Goldenrod, Arrow-leaved Tearthumb, Purple-leaved Willow Herb, Turtlehead, Flat-topped Aster, Common Elder (near end of bloom), Pale-leaved Sunflower (many in one area), Cowwheat (near end of bloom), Tall White Lettuce, Horse Balm [Richweed, Stoneroot], Wintergreen [Checkerberry], Indian Pipe [Corpse Plant], Helleborine, Agrimony (many in spots), Daisy Fleabane [Sweet Scabious], Spotted Joe-Pye Weed

Late Season: Wintergreen [Checkerberry], Cowwheat, Sharp-leaved [Mountain, Whorled] Aster, Sweet-scented Water Lily (white), Meadowsweet, Spotted Touch-me-not [Jewelweed], Agrimony (many in spots), Pink Knotweed [Pinkweed], White Wood Aster, Sweet Viburnum [Nannyberry] (near end of bloom), Pale-leaved Sunflower, Panicled Hawkweed, Enchanter's Nightshade, Helleborine, Horse Balm [Richweed, Stoneroot], Indian Pipe [Corpse Plant], Fringed Loosestrife,

White Avens, Purple-flowering Raspberry, Daisy Fleabane
[Sweet Scabious], Buttercup, Spotted Joe-Pye Weed, Tall
Rattlesnake Root [Gall-of-the-earth]

Pleasant Valley

<u>Wildflower garden</u> *Early Season*: Wild Monkshood, White
Snakeroot

<u>Path to Pike's Pond Trail including wildflower garden</u>
See Trail Information for directions.

Late Season: Feverfew, Common Evening Primrose, Yellow
Avens, Oswego Tea [Bee Balm], Day Lily, Wild Radish,
Spiked Lobelia, Spotted Knapweed, Bladder Campion,
Common Mullein, Yarrow [Milfoil], Lady's Thumb

<u>Pike's Pond Trail</u> *Early Season*: Meadowsweet, Goldenrod,
Agrimony, White Snakeroot, Wild Bergamot (many in one
area), Common St. Johnswort, Spotted Joe-Pye Weed,
Virgin's Bower (many in several areas), Purple Loosestrife
(many), Small White Aster, Daisy Fleabane [Sweet Scabious],
Water Horhound, Boneset [Thoroughwort] (beginning to
bloom), Smaller Forget-me-not, Black-eyed Susan, White
Wood Aster (beginning to bloom), Spotted Touch-me-not
[Jewelweed] , Common Cattail, Large-leaved Aster (beginning
to bloom), Horse Balm [Richweed, Stoneroot], Spiked
Lobelia, Buttercup, Turtlehead, Buttonbush (near end of
bloom), Purple-stemmed Aster (beginning to bloom)

Late Season: Meadowsweet, Goldenrod, Common St. Johnswort, Agrimony, Garden Valerian [Garden Heliotrope] (near end of bloom), Wild Bergamot (many), Spotted Joe-Pye Weed, Fringed Loosestrife (few), Virgin's Bower, Enchanter's Nightshade, Nipplewort, Helleborine (few), Purple Loosestrife (many), Daisy Fleabane [Sweet Scabious], Purple-flowering Raspberry, Lesser Daisy Fleabane, Smaller Forget-me-not, Buttercup, Black-eyed Susan, Common Cattail, Swamp Milkweed, Turtlehead, Horse Balm [Richweed, Stoneroot], Blue Vervain (few), Indian Pipe [Corpse Plant] (one)

Honeysuckle Lane   *See Trail Information for directions.*

Early Season: White Snakeroot, Spotted Touch-me-not [Jewelweed], Common St. Johnswort, Purple Loosestrife, Fringed Loosestrife, Common Burdock, Daisy Fleabane [Sweet Scabious], Garden Loosestrife (near end of bloom), Wild Basil, Buttercup (few), Common Evening Primrose, Tall Nettle

Late Season: Common St. Johnswort, Fringed Loosestrife, Spotted Joe-Pye Weed, Spotted Touch-me-not [Jewelweed], Purple Loosestrife, Yellow Avens, Agrimony, Garden Valerian [Garden Heliotrope] (near end of bloom), Buttercup (one), Common Evening Primrose, Purple-flowering Raspberry, Wild Bergamot (one)

Path to Bluebird Trail *See Trail Information for directions.*

Early Season: Purple Loosestrife, Wild Monkshood, White Snakeroot, Hoary Alyssum, Meadowsweet, Goldenrod, Bladder Campion, Yarrow [Milfoil], Orange Hawkweed [Devil's Paintbrush]

Path to Bluebird Trail including wildflower garden
Late Season: Feverfew, Common Evening Primrose, Day Lily, Oswego Tea [Bee Balm], Common Mullein, Spiked Lobelia, Spotted Knapweed, Wild Radish (many), Lady's Thumb (many), Wild Carrot [Queen Anne's Lace, Bird's Nest], Black-eyed Susan, Common St. Johnswort, Yarrow [Milfoil], Bladder Campion, Meadowsweet

Bluebird Trail *Early Season*: White Wood Aster (beginning to bloom), Meadowsweet, Spiked Lobelia

Late Season: Goldenrod, Meadowsweet, Nipplewort, Buttercup, Yarrow [Milfoil], Common St. Johnswort

Yokun Trail to right *Early Season*: Helleborine, Purple Loosestrife, Meadowsweet, Silverrod (beginning to bloom), Spatterdock [Yellow Pond Lily, Cow Lily]

Late Season: Helleborine, Indian Pipe [Corpse Plant] (one), Meadowsweet, Purple Loosestrife, Daisy Fleabane [Sweet Scabious], Common Cattail, Steeplebush [Hardhack]

Old Wood Road to left *Early Season*: Common Arrowhead, Spotted St. Johnswort, Agrimony

Late Season: Meadowsweet, Spotted St. Johnswort (quite a few in one spot), Agrimony

<u>Beaver Lodge Trail to left</u>   *Early Season*: Goldenrod, Buttercup, Virgin's Bower, Boneset [Thoroughwort], Spotted Joe-Pye Weed (few), Common Cattail

Late Season: Agrimony, Purple Loosestrife, Buttercup (few), Enchanter's Nightshade (few), White Avens (few), Meadowsweet, Common Cattail

<u>Bluebird Trail to left (twice</u>) *Early Season*: No new flowers. *Late Season:* Purple Loosestrife, Spotted Joe-Pye Weed, Spotted Touch-me-not [Jewelweed], Helleborine (one)

Arrowhead
See Trail Information for directions to Wildflower Garden.

<u>Wildflower Garden</u> *Early Season*: Garden Valerian [Garden Heliotrope] (near end of bloom), Pale Dogwood, Wild Carrot [Queen Anne's Lace, Bird's Nest], Daisy Fleabane [Sweet Scabious], Creeping Bellflower, Bladder Campion, Black-eyed Susan, Turk's-cap Lily (near end of bloom), White Wood Aster, Great Lobelia

Late Season: Hydrangea, Garden [European] Columbine, Black-eyed Susan, Herb Robert, Bladder Campion, Garden Valerian [Garden Heliotrope] (near end of bloom), Daisy Fleabane [Sweet Scabious], Creeping Bellflower, Oxeye Daisy, Day Lily (yellow), Cow [Tufted] Vetch, Wild Carrot [Queen Anne's Lace, Bird's Nest], Black Snakeroot [Black Cohosh], Silky Dogwood (near end of bloom), Fringed Loosestrife, Turk's-cap Lily

<u>Area to left of Wildflower Garden</u>   *Early Season*: Musk
Mallow, Goldenrod, Hedge Bindweed (light pink), Cow
[Tufted] Vetch

Late Season: Hedge Bindweed, Wild Carrot [Queen Anne's
Lace, Bird's Nest], Rugosa Rose, Black-eyed Susan, Musk
Mallow, Garden Valerian [Garden Heliotrope], Daisy Fleabane
[Sweet Scabious]

<u>Left of driveway</u> *Late Season:* Day Lily (orange*)*, Birdsfoot
Trefoil

Canoe Meadows

<u>Sacred Way Trail</u>   *See Trail Information for directions.*

Early Season: White Campion, Goldenrod, Meadowsweet,
Panicled Aster (beginning to bloom), Spotted Touch-me-not
[Jewelweed] (many in spots), Wild Balsam Apple [Wild
Cucumber], Purple Loosestrife (many in areas), Spotted Joe-
Pye Weed (quite a few), Turtlehead, Arrow-leaved Tearthumb,
Common Arrowhead, Hedge Bindweed, Tall [Green-headed]
Coneflower, Virgin's Bower (many in spots), Daisy Fleabane
[Sweet Scabious], Maiden Pink, Fringed Loosestrife,
Agrimony, Panicled Hawkweed, White Wood Aster, Zigzag
[Broad-leaved] Goldenrod, Indian Pipe [Corpse Plant],
Common St. Johnswort, Marsh Skullcap, Bittersweet
Nightshade, Tall Nettle, Butter-and-eggs, Motherwort (near
end of bloom), Pink Knotweed [Pinkweed], Blue Vervain,
Swamp Milkweed, Canada Thistle

Late Season: Cow [Tufted] Vetch, Meadowsweet (quite a few), Goldenrod, Daisy Fleabane [Sweet Scabious], Common Evening Primrose, Yarrow [Milfoil], Purple Loosestrife (many), Bladder Campion, Buttercup, Fringed Loosestrife, Wild Balsam Apple [Wild Cucumber], Spotted Joe-Pye Weed (quite a few), Hedge Bindweed, Spotted Touch-me-not [Jewelweed] (many), Common Arrowhead, Smaller Forget-me-not, Tall [Green] Coneflower, Common St. Johnswort, Spatterdock [Yellow Pond Lily, Meadow Lily], Maiden Pink, Agrimony, Panicled Hawkweed, Swamp Milkweed, Blue Vervain, Bittersweet Nightshade, Butter-and-eggs, Arrow-leaved Tearthumb

Road   *See Trail Information for directions.*

Early Season: Daisy Fleabane [Sweet Scabious], Bladder Campion, Cow [Tufted] Vetch, Butter-and-eggs, Hoary Alyssum, White Campion, Wild Balsam Apple [Wild Cucumber], Alfalfa [Lucerne] (many in one area), Spotted Touch-me-not [Jewelweed] (many), Hedge Bindweed, Canada Thistle, Tall Nettle, Common Burdock (many in one area), Goldenrod, Bouncing Bet [Soapwort], Pokeweed, Motherwort (near end of bloom), White Campion, White Snakeroot, Cup Plant [Indian Cup] (many on one spot), Fringed Loosestrife, Panicled Aster (beginning to bloom), Wild Hydrangea, Flat-topped Aster, Spatterdock [Yellow Pond Lily, Cow Lily], Purple Loosestrife (many), Pale Dogwood, Blue Vervain, Spotted Joe-Pye Weed, Sharp-leaved [Whorled, Mountain] Aster (beginning to bloom), Wintergreen [Checkerberry], White Wood Aster (beginning to bloom), Meadowsweet, Turtlehead, Tall [Green-headed] Coneflower, Virgin's Bower, Buttercup, Boneset [Thoroughwort] (many in one area), Panicled Aster (beginning to bloom)

Late Season: Daisy Fleabane [Sweet Scabious], Silvery Cinquefoil, Cow [Tufted] Vetch, Alfalfa [Lucerne] (many - purple and blue), Hoary Alyssum, Bladder Campion, White Campion (many), Goldenrod, Meadowsweet, Wild Carrot [Queen Anne's Lace, Bird's Nest], Canada Thistle, Yarrow [Milfoil], Agrimony, Common Burdock, Bouncing Bet [Soapwort], Buttercup, Wild Balsam Apple [Wild Cucumber], Tall Nettle, Spotted Touch-me-not [Jewelweed], Enchanter's Nightshade, Fringed Loosestrife, Wild Basil, Virgin's Bower, Nodding [Pale, Dock-leaved] Smartweed, Hedge Mustard, Wild Hydrangea, Dame's Violet [Dame's Rocket] (near end of bloom), Common Evening Primrose, Motherwort, Cup Plant [Indian Cup], Spatterdock [Yellow Pond Lily, Cow Lily], Spotted Joe-Pye Weed, Helleborine, Maiden Pink, Common St. Johnswort, Centaury (many in one place), Boneset [Thoroughwort], Swamp Smartweed, Schreber's Aster (quite a few)

<u>Wolf Pine Trail</u>   *Early Season*: Tall [Green-headed] Coneflower, Wild Balsam Apple [Wild Cucumber], Spotted Joe-Pye Weed, Spotted Touch-me-not [Jewelweed], Heart-leaved Aster (beginning to bloom), Indian Pipe [Corpse Plant], Dame's Violet [Dame's Rocket], Daisy Fleabane [Sweet Scabious], White Snakeroot, Yarrow [Milfoil]

Late Season: Buttercup (few), White Avens (few), Agrimony (quite a few), Daisy Fleabane [Sweet Scabious], Helleborine (one), Indian Pipe [Corpse Plant], Dame's Violet [Dame's Rocket] (one - near end of bloom)

Trails across from Hancock Shaker Village
See Trail Information for directions.

Road through field   *Early Season*: Common St. Johnswort,
Yarrow [Milfoil] (many), Oxeye Daisy, Meadowsweet (quite
a few), Goldenrod (quite a few), Daisy Fleabane [Sweet
Scabious], Field Hawkweed [King Devil], Wild Carrot [Queen
Anne's Lace, Bird's Nest], Spotted St. Johnswort, New
England Aster, Bladder Campion, Steeplebush [Hardhack],
Orange Hawkweed [Devil's Paintbrush], Wild Radish, Spotted
Joe-Pye Weed (many), Virgin's Bower, Common Evening
Primrose, Boneset [Thoroughwort] (many in one area),
Spotted Touch-me-not [Jewelweed] (many in spots), Butter-
and-eggs

Late Season: Yarrow [Milfoil], Maiden Pink, Silvery
Cinquefoil, Wild Carrot [Queen Anne's Lace, Bird's Nest],
Oxeye Daisy, Meadowsweet, Common St. Johnswort, Spiked
Lobelia, Daisy Fleabane [Sweet Scabious], Common Evening
Primrose, Wild Radish (white - one), Rough Cinquefoil,
Virgin's Bower, Goldenrod, Spotted Joe-Pye Weed, Boneset
[Thoroughwort], Spotted Touch-me-not [Jewelweed],
Common Mullein, Steeplebush [Hardhack] (few), Black-eyed
Susan (few)

Road to right through woods   *Early Season*: A few flowers
listed in field plus White Vervain, Indian Pipe [Corpse Plant],
Fringed Loosestrife, White Wood Aster, Sharp-leaved
[Mountain, Whorled] Aster (many in places), Purple-flowering
Raspberry, Tall White Lettuce, Hog Peanut (white and violet-
beginning to bloom), Panicled Hawkweed, White Avens (near
end of bloom), Agrimony, Helleborine

Late Season: Wild Basil, Agrimony, Fringed Loosestrife, Spotted Touch-me-not [Jewelweed], Helleborine, Spiked Lobelia, Spikenard, Purple-flowering Raspberry (quite a few), Celandine, Panicled Hawkweed, Tall Nettle, White Avens, Enchanter's Nightshade (near end of bloom), Indian Pipe [Corpse Plant] (few), Buttercup, Sharp-leaved [Mountain, Whorled] Aster

Road past field toward highway *Early Season*: Some flowers listed before plus Wild Basil, Purple-leaved Willow Herb, Arrow-leaved Tearthumb, Oxeye Daisy, Calico [Starved] Aster, Small White Aster

Late Season: Spotted Touch-me-not [Jewelweed], Wild Basil, Daisy Fleabane [Sweet Scabious], Meadowsweet, Buttercup (few), Spotted St. Johnswort, Agrimony, Goldenrod, Spotted Joe-Pye Weed, Fringed Loosestrife (near end of bloom)

Path around Shaker reservoir *Late Season:* Yarrow [Milfoil], Meadowsweet (many), Common Cattail, Goldenrod, Steeplebush [Hardhack] (few), Spotted Joe-Pye Weed, Buttercup (one), Common St. Johnswort, Common Evening Primrose, Spotted St. Johnswort (quite a few), Spiked Lobelia, (few), Black-eyed Susan, Hedge Bindweed, Enchanter's Nightshade, Purple-flowering Raspberry, Northern Bugleweed, Narrow-leaved Mountain Mint, Agrimony, Wild Bergamot, Daisy Fleabane [Sweet Scabious]

LAST TWO WEEKS IN AUGUST

Benedict Pond
See Trail Information for directions.

<u>Path to Pond Loop Trail (beginning at left of swimming area)</u>
Early Season: White Wood Aster (many in places on trail), Lowrie's Aster, Calico [Starved] Aster, Silverrod, Spreading Dogbane, Goldenrod

Late Season: White Wood Aster, Goldenrod, Schreber's Aster, Round-leaved Dogwood (near end of bloom), Silverrod, Cowwheat, Bladder Campion (near end of bloom), Bush Honeysuckle

<u>Pond Loop Trail to left</u> *Early Season*: Some flowers listed on Path to Trail plus Sharp-leaved [Mountain, Whorled] Aster (many in spots), Spotted Touch-me-not [Jewelweed] (many in spots), Turtlehead (white), Boneset [Thoroughwort], Sweet-scented Water Lily (white), Purple-stemmed Aster, Pale-leaved Sunflower (many in spots), Arrow-leaved Tearthumb, Northern Bugleweed, Flat-topped Aster (many in spots), Tall White Lettuce, Horse Balm [Richweed, Stoneroot] (near end of bloom), Small White Aster, White Snakeroot, Hog Peanut (violet), Schreber's Aster, Agrimony, Lady's Thumb, Spotted Joe-Pye Weed (near end of bloom)

Late Season: White Wood Aster (many), Spreading Dogbane, Goldenrod, Yarrow [Milfoil], Sharp-leaved [Mountain, Whorled] Aster, Turtlehead, Large-leaved Aster, Indian Pipe [Corpse Plant], Sweet-scented Water Lily (white), Pale-leaved Sunflower, Spotted Touch-me-not [Jewelweed], Arrow-leaved Tearthumb, Boneset [Thoroughwort], Blue-stemmed [Wreath] Goldenrod, Cowwheat, Spiked Lobelia, Hog Peanut (near end of bloom), Purple-flowering Raspberry (near end of bloom), Tall Rattlesnake Root [Gall-of-the-earth], Buttercup (one), Flat-topped Aster, Spotted St. Johnswort, Panicled Hawkweed, Meadowsweet, Horse Balm [Richweed, Stoneroot], Helleborine, Agrimony, Spotted Joe-Pye Weed

Pleasant Valley

<u>Near entrance</u>   *Early Season*: Thin-leaved Sunflower

<u>Path to Pike's Pond Trail including wildflower garden</u>
See Trail Information for directions.

Early Season: White Snakeroot, Spotted Touch-me-not [Jewelweed], Wild Monkshood

Late Season: Great Lobelia, Common St. Johnswort, Spiked Lobelia, Wild Monkshood, White Snakeroot, Oswego Tea [Bee Balm], Purple Bergamot, Oxeye Daisy (near end of bloom), Goldenrod, Wild Radish, Common Mullein

<u>Pike's Pond Trail</u> *Early Season*: White Snakeroot (many in spots), White Wood Aster (many in spots), Goldenrod, Garden Valerian [Garden Heliotrope] (near end of bloom), Spotted Touch-me-not [Jewelweed], Spotted Joe-Pye Weed, Virgin's Bower (near end of bloom), Wild Bergamot (near end of bloom), Purple Loosestrife, Purple-stemmed Aster, Boneset [Thoroughwort], Calico [Starved] Aster, Agrimony, Heart-leaved Aster, Hog Peanut (light lilac-near end of bloom), Northern Bugleweed, Common St. Johnswort (near end of bloom), Meadowsweet (near end of bloom), Silverrod, Lowrie's Aster, Spiked Lobelia (near end of bloom), Sharp-leaved [Whorled, Mountain] Aster, Panicled Hawkweed (near

end of bloom), Horse Balm, [Richweed, Stoneroot], Tall
White Lettuce, Turtlehead

Late Season: Meadowsweet, Bull Thistle, Yarrow [Milfoil]
(near end of bloom), Garden Valerian [Garden Heliotrope],
Wild Bergamot, Spotted Joe-Pye Weed, Virgin's Bower
(many), Common St. Johnswort, Buttercup (few), Purple
Loosestrife, Goldenrod, Purple-stemmed Aster,
Meadowsweet, Agrimony, Smaller Forget-me-not, Spotted
Touch-me-not [Jewelweed], Common Cattail, Boneset
[Thoroughwort], Schreber's Aster (one), White Wood Aster,
Horse Balm [Richweed, Stoneroot], Large-leaved Aster (one),
White Snakeroot

Honeysuckle Lane *See Trail Information for directions.*

Late Season: Spotted Touch-me-not [Jewelweed], Common
St. Johnswort, Goldenrod, Purple Loosestrife, Silky Dogwood
(near end of bloom), Common Evening Primrose, Agrimony,
Garden Valerian [Garden Heliotrope] (near end of bloom),
Peppermint, Spiked Lobelia, White Snakeroot, Common
Burdock, Virgin's Bower, Purple-flowering Raspberry

Path to Bluebird Trail including wildflower garden
See Trail Information for directions.

Early Season: White Snakeroot, Spotted Touch-me-not
[Jewelweed], Wild Monkshood, Goldenrod, Bladder
Campion, Meadowsweet

Late Season: Pale-leaved Sunflower, White Snakeroot, Wild
Monkshood, Common St. Johnswort, Great Lobelia, Oswego
Tea [Bee Balm], Purple Bergamot, Spiked Lobelia, Maiden
Pink, Wild Radish, Common Mullein, Lady's Thumb,

Goldenrod, Wild Carrot [Queen Anne's Lace, Bird's Nest], Meadowsweet, Bladder Campion, Yarrow [Milfoil]

Bluebird Trail to left *Early Season*: Some flowers mentioned on Path to Trail plus White Wood Aster

Late Season: Meadowsweet, Goldenrod, Common St. Johnswort, White Wood Aster

Yokun Trail to right *Early Season*: A few flowers listed on Path to Trail and Bluebird Trail plus Common Cattail, Silverrod, Purple Loosestrife (near end of bloom), Small White Aster

Late Season: White Wood Aster, Spotted Joe-Pye Weed, Purple Loosestrife, Common Cattail, Spiked Lobelia, Spatterdock [Yellow Pond Lily, Cow Lily], Silverrod, Virgin's Bower, White Snakeroot

Old Wood Road to left *Early Season*: A few flowers listed on previous trails plus Calico [Starved] Aster, Spotted Joe-Pye Weed (near end of bloom), Common Arrowhead, Closed Gentian, Heart-leaved Aster, Tall White Lettuce

Late Season: White Wood Aster, Purple Loosestrife, Common Cattail, Spotted St. Johnswort, Spotted Joe-Pye Weed, Bittersweet Nightshade

Beaver Lodge Trail to left *Early Season*: A few flowers listed on previous trails plus Buttercup, Boneset [Thoroughwort], Blue Vervain, Panicled Hawkweed

Late Season: Meadowsweet (near end of bloom), Goldenrod, White Snakeroot (few), Purple Loosestrife (many in spots), Boneset [Thoroughwort] (few), Common Cattail, Spotted Joe-Pye Weed (few), Common Arrowhead (one)

<u>Bluebird Trail to left (twic)e</u> *Early Season*: No new flowers.

Late Season: Spotted Touch-me-not [Jewelweed]

Arrowhead
See Trail Information for directions to Wildflower Garden.

<u>Wildflower Garden</u> *Early Season*: White Wood Aster (quite a few), Bladder Campion, Garden Valerian [Garden Heliotrope] (near end of bloom), Great Lobelia (few), Wild Carrot [Queen Anne's Lace, Bird's Nest] (few), Black-eyed Susan, Daisy Fleabane [Sweet Scabious]

Late Season: Black-eyed Susan, Wild Carrot [Queen Anne's Lace, Bird's Nest], Day Lily (yellow), Goldenrod, Silky Dogwood (near end of bloom), Hydrangea, Daisy Fleabane [Sweet Scabious], White Wood Aster, Fringed Loosestrife, Spotted Joe-Pye Weed (near end of bloom), Bladder Campion

<u>Area to left of Wildflower Garden</u> *Early Season*: Goldenrod, Hedge Bindweed, Musk Mallow, Bull Thistle

Late Season: Wild Carrot [Queen Anne's Lace, Bird's Nest], Hedge Bindweed, Musk Mallow

Canoe Meadows

Sacred Way Trail   *See Trail Information for directions.*

Early Season: Butter-and-eggs, Goldenrod (many), Panicled Aster, Meadowsweet (near end of bloom), Yarrow [Milfoil], Fringed Loosestrife, Spotted Touch-me-not [Jewelweed] (many), Purple Loosestrife (many), Arrow-leaved Tearthumb (many), Wild Balsam Apple [Wild Cucumber] (many), Spotted Joe-Pye Weed (quite a few), Hedge Bindweed (quite a few), Tall Nettle, Turtlehead, Common Arrowhead, Bittersweet Nightshade, Tall [Green-headed] Coneflower, Daisy Fleabane [Sweet Scabious], Virgin's Bower, Sweet Everlasting [Catfoot] (few), Maiden Pink (few), Agrimony, Lowrie's Aster, White Wood Aster (many), Goldenrod, Panicled Hawkweed, Zigzag [Broad-leaved] Goldenrod, White Snakeroot, Indian Pipe [Corpse Plant], Mad-dog Skullcap, Blue Vervain (few), Tansy (few), Northern Willow Herb

Late Season: Goldenrod, Cow [Tufted] Vetch, Meadowsweet (near end of bloom), Common Evening Primrose, Daisy Fleabane [Sweet Scabious], Spotted Joe-Pye Weed, Purple Loosestrife (many), Spotted Touch-me-not [Jewelweed], Silky Dogwood (near end of bloom), Wild Balsam Apple [Wild Cucumber], Turtlehead, Smaller Forget-me-not, Common Arrowhead, Blue Vervain, Tall [Green-headed] Coneflower, Virgin's Bower, Hedge Bindweed, Maiden Pink, New England Aster, Yarrow [Milfoil] (near end of bloom), Pearly Everlasting, Fringed Loosestrife, Spiked Lobelia (few), Panicled Hawkweed (few), White Wood Aster, Buttercup (few), Purple-stemmed Aster (beginning to bloom), Agrimony, Canada Thistle, Butter-and-eggs, Swamp Milkweed

<u>Road</u>   *See Trail Information for directions.*

Early Season: Daisy Fleabane [Sweet Scabious], Bladder Campion, Alfalfa [Lucerne], Hoary Alyssum, Butter-and-eggs, Cow [Tufted] Vetch, White Campion, Wild Balsam Apple [Wild Cucumber], Bouncing Bet [Soapwort] , Spotted Touch-me-not [Jewelweed] (many), Tall Nettle, Buttercup, Lowrie's Aster, Cup Plant [Indian Cup], Goldenrod, Wild Carrot [Queen Anne's Lace, Bird's Nest], Flat-topped Aster, Hog Peanut (lilac and light lilac), Purple Loosestrife, Common Cattail, Calico [Starved] Aster, Lady's Thumb (few), Sharp-leaved [Whorled, Mountain] Aster, Small White Aster, Yarrow [Milfoil] (near end of bloom), White Snakeroot, Spotted Joe-Pye Weed, Tall [Green-headed] Coneflower, Virgin's Bower, New England Aster, Boneset [Thoroughwort], Panicled Aster, Meadowsweet (near end of bloom)

Late Season: Daisy Fleabane [Sweet Scabious], Bladder Campion, Alfalfa [Lucerne] (many), Hoary Alyssum, Butter-and-eggs, Goldenrod, Meadowsweet, Wild Carrot [Queen Anne's Lace, Bird's Nest], Cow [Tufted] Vetch, Canada Thistle (near end of bloom), Wild Balsam Apple [Wild Cucumber], Yarrow [Milfoil] (near end of bloom), Common Burdock, Agrimony, Purple Loosestrife, Bouncing Bet [Soapwort], Tall Nettle (many in one spot), Spotted Touch-me-not [Jewelweed] (many), Fringed Loosestrife (quite a few), Spotted Joe-Pye Weed, Wild Hydrangea, Lady's Thumb, Motherwort, Nipplewort, Cup Plant [Indian Cup] (many), Maiden Pink, Flat-topped Aster, Buttercup (few), Common Cattail, Sharp-leaved [Mountain, Whorled] Aster, White Snakeroot, Pink Knotweed [Pinkweed], Silky Dogwood (near end of bloom), Virgin's Bower (many in one spot), Boneset [Thoroughwort], Gray-headed Coneflower (few), Schreber's Aster

<u>Wolf Pine Trail</u>   *Early Season*: Goldenrod, Spotted Touch-me-not [Jewelweed] (many in spots), Heart-leaved Aster (few), Daisy Fleabane [Sweet Scabious] (few), White Snakeroot (few), White Wood Aster (few)

Late Season: Agrimony, Spotted Touch-me-not [Jewelweed], Wild Hydrangea, Dame's Violet [Dame's Rocket], Indian Pipe [Corpse Plant] (quite a few in one place), White Campion (one), Daisy Fleabane [Sweet Scabious] (few)

Trails across from Hancock Shaker Village
See Trail Information for directions.

<u>Road through field</u>   *Early Season*: Goldenrod (many), Yarrow [Milfoil] (quite a few), Wild Carrot [Queen Anne's Lace, Bird's Nest], Meadowsweet, Orange Hawkweed [Devil's Paintbrush], New England Aster, Bladder Campion, Field Hawkweed [King Devil], Lady's Thumb, Spotted Joe-Pye Weed, Arrow-leaved Tearthumb, Spotted Touch-me-not [Jewelweed] (many in spots), Boneset [Thoroughwort] (quite a few in spots), Daisy Fleabane [Sweet Scabious], Lowrie's Aster

Late Season: Meadowsweet, Daisy Fleabane [Sweet Scabious], Yarrow [Milfoil], Wild Carrot [Queen Anne's Lace, Bird's Nest], Goldenrod, Steeplebush [Hardhack], Bladder Campion, Common St. Johnswort (near end of bloom), Wild Mint, Common Evening Primrose, Smaller White Snakeroot, Boneset [Thoroughwort], Spotted Joe-Pye Weed, Maiden Pink, Oxeye Daisy (near end of bloom), Common Mullein, Cup Plant [Indian Cup], Spotted Touch-me-not [Jewelweed], Lady's Thumb

Road to right through woods *Early Season*: Spotted Touch-me-not [Jewelweed] (many in spots), Goldenrod, White Vervain, Swamp Smartweed, Meadowsweet, White Wood Aster (many), Daisy Fleabane [Sweet Scabious], White Snakeroot, Zigzag [Broad-leaved] Goldenrod, Sharp-leaved [Mountain, Whorled] Aster (many in spots), Common Burdock, Hog Peanut (white, light lilac), Spiked Lobelia, Tall Nettle, Tall White Lettuce, Purple-flowering Raspberry

Late Season: Spiked Lobelia, Spotted Touch-me-not [Jewelweed], White Wood Aster, Sharp-leaved [Mountain, Whorled] Aster, Daisy Fleabane [Sweet Scabious], Fringed Loosestrife, Purple-leaved Willow Herb, Common Burdock, Turtlehead, Purple-flowering Raspberry, Panicled Hawkweed

Road past field toward highway *Early Season*: Lady's Thumb, Common Smartweed [Water Pepper], Arrow-leaved Tearthumb, Beggar Ticks [Sticktight], Spotted Joe-Pye Weed, Meadowsweet, Buttercup, Calico [Starved] Aster, Small White Aster (beginning to bloom)

Late Season: Spotted Touch-me-not [Jewelweed] (quite a few), White Wood Aster, Buttercup (few), Daisy Fleabane [Sweet Scabious], Oxeye Daisy (few), Goldenrod, Arrow-leaved Tearthumb, Purple-leaved Willow Herb, Common St. Johnswort, Hog Peanut, Schreber's Aster

Path partway around Shaker reservoir *Early Season*: Calico [Starved] Aster, Yarrow [Milfoil], White Wood Aster, Goldenrod, Spotted Joe-Pye Weed, Spotted Touch-me-not [Jewelweed], Closed [Bottle] Gentian, Wild Mint, Daisy Fleabane [Sweet Scabious], Meadowsweet, New England Aster, Black-eyed Susan, Silverrod, Common Arrowhead, Arrow-leaved Tearthumb, Narrow-leaved Mountain Mint

Late Season: White Wood Aster, Meadowsweet (near end of bloom), Spotted Touch-me-not [Jewelweed], Purple-leaved Willow Herb, Calico [Starved] Aster, Turtlehead, Goldenrod, Yarrow [Milfoil], Spotted St. Johnswort, Spotted Joe-Pye Weed, Wild Mint, Arrow-leaved Tearthumb, Spiked Lobelia, Boneset [Thoroughwort], Black-eyed Susan, Virgin's Bower, Common Evening Primrose, Daisy Fleabane [Sweet Scabious], Narrow-leaved Mountain Mint

FIRST TWO WEEKS IN SEPTEMBER

Benedict Pond
See Trail Information for directions.

<u>Path to Pond Loop Trail (beginning at left of swimming area)</u>
Early Season: Calico [Starved] Aster, White Wood Aster, Lowrie's Aster, Heart-leaved Aster, Smooth Aster, Silverrod

Late Season: White Wood Aster (many), Goldenrod, Heart-leaved Aster, Silverrod (quite a few)

<u>Pond Loop Trail to left</u>   *Early Season:* Sharp-leaved [Mountain, Whorled] Aster (many in spots), White Wood Aster (many in spots), Purple-stemmed Aster, Spotted Touch-me-not [Jewelweed], Wintergreen [Checkerberry], Blue-stemmed [Wreath] Goldenrod (quite a few in places), Tall White Lettuce, Turtlehead, Sweet-scented Water Lily (white), Goldenrod, Flat-topped Aster, Panicled Aster, White Snakeroot, Schreber's Aster, Hog Peanut (white), Small White Aster

Late Season: White Wood Aster (many), Heart-leaved Aster, Silverrod, Goldenrod, Sharp-leaved [Mountain, Whorled] Aster, Turtlehead, Purple-stemmed Aster, Arrow-leaved Tearthumb, Spotted Touch-me-not [Jewelweed], Flat-topped Aster (many in one area), Small White Aster, Pale-leaved Sunflower, Northern Willow Herb, Boneset [Thoroughwort] (near end of bloom), Tall White Lettuce, Blue-stemmed [Wreath] Goldenrod, Panicled Aster, Large-leaved Aster, Sweet-scented Water Lily (white), Panicled Hawkweed, Swamp Smartweed, Horse Balm [Richweed, Stoneroot], Agrimony (near end of bloom), Hog Peanut, Tall Rattlesnake root [Gall-of-the-earth], Lowrie's Aster

Pleasant Valley

<u>Near entrance</u> *Late Season:* Heart-leaved Aster, Thin-leaved Sunflower, Wild Carrot [Queen Anne's Lace, Bird's Nest], White Snakeroot (many)

<u>Path to Pike's Pond Trail including wildflower garden</u>
See Trail Information for directions.

Early Season: White Snakeroot, Spotted Touch-me-not [Jewelweed], Great Lobelia, Bull Thistle, Goldenrod, Meadowsweet, Agrimony

Late Season: Spotted Touch-me-not [Jewelweed] (many), White Snakeroot, Great Lobelia, Common Burdock, Daisy Fleabane [Sweet Scabious], Oswego Tea [Bee Balm], Wild Monkshood, Feverfew, Purple Bergamot (near end of bloom), Bull Thistle, Goldenrod (many), White Wood Aster, Buttercup, Black-eyed Susan, Spiked Lobelia (near end of bloom), Chicory (one), Spotted Joe-Pye Weed, Spotted Knapweed, White Sweet Clover, Common Evening Primrose

<u>Pike's Pond Trail</u> *Early Season*: White Snakeroot (many in spots), Goldenrod, Panicled Aster, Purple-stemmed Aster, Purple Loosestrife, Small White Aster, Calico [Starved] Aster, Daisy Fleabane [Sweet Scabious], Lowrie's Aster, Heart-leaved Aster, Peppermint, White Wood Aster (many in spots), Silverrod, Schreber's Aster, Horse Balm [Richweed, Stoneroot], Tall White Lettuce, Blue-stemmed [Wreath] Goldenrod, Common Cattail, Nodding Bur Marigold, Sharp-leaved [Mountain, Whorled] Aster

Late Season: White Snakeroot, Wild Bergamot (near end of bloom), Goldenrod (many), Spotted Touch-me-not, [Jewelweed], Spotted Joe-Pye Weed (near end of bloom), Garden Valerian [Garden Heliotrope] (near end of bloom), Nipplewort, Purple Loosestrife (few), Smaller Forget-me-not, Virginia Bugleweed, Agrimony, Boneset [Thoroughwort], Heart-leaved Aster, Peppermint (beginning to bloom), Small White Aster, Common Cattail, Narrow-leaved Cattail, Calico [Starved] Aster, Common St. Johnswort, Tall White Lettuce, Silverrod, Horse Balm [Richweed, Stoneroot], Turtlehead, Panicled Aster (beginning to bloom), Sharp-leaved [Mountain, Whorled] Aster, Purple-stemmed Aster

<u>Honeysuckle Lane</u>   *See Trail Information for directions.*

Early Season: White Snakeroot (many), Spotted Touch-me-not [Jewelweed] (many), Purple-stemmed Aster, Panicled Aster, Goldenrod (many), Calico [Starved] Aster, Thin-leaved Sunflower

Late Season: Spotted Touch-me-not [Jewelweed] (many), Goldenrod, Common Burdock (near end of bloom), White Snakeroot (many), Daisy Fleabane [Sweet Scabious], Purple-flowering Raspberry (one)

<u>Path to Bluebird Trail including wildflower garden</u>
See Trail Information for directions.

Early Season: White Snakeroot, Spotted Touch-me-not [Jewelweed], Great Lobelia, Bull Thistle, Goldenrod, Meadowsweet, Agrimony, Bladder Campion

Late Season: Goldenrod (many in places), White Snakeroot (many in places), Great Lobelia, Common Burdock, Daisy Fleabane [Sweet Scabious], Oswego Tea [Bee Balm], Spotted Touch-me-not [Jewelweed], Purple Bergamot (near end of bloom), Wild Monkshood, Feverfew, Bull Thistle, White Wood Aster (few), Canada Thistle (few), Spiked Lobelia (near end of bloom), Panicled Aster (beginning to bloom), Yarrow [Milfoil] (few - near end of bloom), White Sweet Clover (few), Lady's Thumb, Bladder Campion, Oxeye Daisy (few), Wild Radish (few)

<u>Bluebird Trail</u>   *Early Season*: Goldenrod, Calico [Starved] Aster

Late Season: Small White Aster, Nipplewort (near end of bloom), Spiked Lobelia, Small White Aster, White Wood Aster, Goldenrod (many), Calico [Starved] Aster, Meadowsweet

<u>Yokun Trail to right</u>   *Early Season*: White Wood Aster, White Snakeroot (many in spots), Tall White Lettuce, Lowrie's Aster, Silverrod, Daisy Fleabane [Sweet Scabious], Heart-leaved Aster

Late Season: White Wood Aster (quite a few), White Snakeroot, Tall White Lettuce, Goldenrod, Small White Aster, Nipplewort, Silverrod, Lowrie's Aster (one), Spotted Touch-me-not [Jewelweed], Heart-leaved Aster

<u>Old Wood Road to left</u>   *Early Season*: Closed [Bottle] Gentian

Late Season: Small White Aster, White Lettuce, White Wood Aster, White Snakeroot, Boneset [Thoroughwort], Purple Loosestrife (near end of bloom), Spotted Joe-Pye Weed (near end of bloom), Closed [Bottle] Gentian, Spotted St. Johnswort, Goldenrod, Heart-leaved Aster, Common Cattail

<u>Beaver Lodge Trail to left</u>   *Early Season*: Panicled Aster

Late Season: White Wood Aster, Small White Aster, Spotted St. Johnswort, Goldenrod, Calico [Starved] Aster, Buttercup, White Snakeroot, Boneset [Thoroughwort], Closed [Bottle] Gentian

<u>Bluebird Trail to left (twice)</u>   *Early Season*: Beggar Ticks [Sticktight], Spotted Touch-me-not [Jewelweed], Turtlehead (near end of bloom), Zigzag [Broad-leaved] Goldenrod

Late Season: Heart-leaved Aster, White Wood Aster, Spotted Touch-me-not [Jewelweed], Goldenrod, Tall White Lettuce, Beggar Ticks [Sticktight]

Arrowhead
See Trail Information for directions to Wildflower Garden.

<u>Wildflower Garden</u>   *Early Season*: White Wood Aster, Panicled Aster, White Snakeroot, Black-eyed Susan, Creeping Bellflower (near end of bloom), Pink Turtlehead, Great Lobelia, Daisy Fleabane [Sweet Scabious], Lowrie's Aster, Heart-leaved Aster

Late Season: Black-eyed Susan, White Wood Aster, Goldenrod, Great Lobelia, Pink Turtlehead, Daisy Fleabane [Sweet Scabious], Bladder Campion, Purple Coneflower, Garden Valerian [Garden Heliotrope] (near end of bloom), Wild Carrot [Queen Anne's Lace, Bird's Nest], Spotted Joe-Pye Weed

<u>Area to left of Garden</u> *Early Season*: Goldenrod, Panicled Aster, Showy Sunflower (many), New England Aster

Late Season: Hedge Bindweed, Rugosa Rose (near end of bloom), Musk Mallow, Goldenrod (many). New England Aster, Showy Sunflower (beginning to bloom), Wild Carrot [Queen Anne's Lace, Bird's Nest]

Canoe Meadows

<u>Sacred Way Trail</u> *See Trail Information for directions.*

Early Season: Panicled Aster (white), Goldenrod (many), Spotted Touch-me-not [Jewelweed] (many in spots), Turtlehead (near end of bloom), Arrow-leaved Tearthumb, Larger Bur Marigold, Spotted Joe-Pye Weed (near end of bloom), Purple Loosestrife (near end of bloom), Tall Nettle, Purple-stemmed Aster, Lowrie's Aster, New England Aster, Pearly Everlasting, Heart-leaved Aster, White Wood Aster (many in spots), Panicled Hawkweed, Zigzag [Broad-leaved] Goldenrod, Small White Aster, White Snakeroot, Meadowsweet (near end of bloom), Panicled Aster (violet-tinged), Beggar Ticks [Sticktight]

Late Season: Goldenrod (many), Panicled Aster (beginning to bloom), Spotted Touch-me-not [Jewelweed] (many), Common St. Johnswort (near end of bloom), Wild Carrot [Queen Anne's Lace, Bird's Nest], Bladder Campion, Turtlehead, Arrow-leaved Tearthumb, Spotted Joe-Pye Weed (near end of bloom - quite a few), Purple Loosestrife (quite a few), Tall [Green-headed] Coneflower, New England Aster, Pearly Everlasting, Heart-leaved Aster, Lowrie's Aster, Common Evening Primrose, Meadowsweet (near end of bloom), Sweet Everlasting [Catfoot], Maiden Pink, Spiked Lobelia (near end of bloom), White Wood Aster, Panicled Hawkweed, Zigzag [Broad-leaved] Goldenrod, White Snakeroot (few), Blue Curls, Buttercup, Purple-stemmed Aster, Small White Aster, Calico [Starved] Aster, Swamp Smartweed, Nodding [Pale, Dock-leaved] Smartweed, Butter-and-eggs, Canada Thistle (near end of bloom), Tansy

<u>Road</u>   *See Trail Information for directions.*

Early Season: Butter-and-eggs, Goldenrod, Panicled Aster (most white, a few violet tinged), Bladder Campion, Hedge Bindweed, Cow [Tufted] Vetch, Spotted Touch-me-not [Jewelweed], Tall Nettle, Bouncing Bet [Soapwort], White Snakeroot, Lowrie's Aster, Daisy Fleabane [Sweet Scabious], White Campion, Small White Aster, Purple-stemmed Aster, Swamp Smartweed, Nodding Bur Marigold (few), Beggar Ticks [Sticktight], Sharp-leaved [Mountain, Whorled] Aster, Heart-leaved Aster (beginning to bloom), White Wood Aster, Tall [Green-headed] Coneflower, New England Aster, Zigzag [Broad-leaved] Goldenrod, Common Evening Primrose

Late Season: Panicled Aster (beginning to bloom), Goldenrod (many), Bladder Campion (many), Butter-and-eggs, White Campion (many), Alfalfa [Lucerne] (beginning to bloom), Spotted Touch-me-not [Jewelweed] (many), Canada Thistle, Common Burdock (near end of bloom), Bouncing Bet [Soapwort], Tall Nettle, Daisy Fleabane [Sweet Scabious], White Snakeroot, Spiked Lobelia, Wood Nettle (few), White Wood Aster, Wild Balsam Apple [Wild Cucumber], Wild Hydrangea, Cup Plant [Indian Cup] (many in one place), Flat-topped Aster, Hog Peanut, Purple Loosestrife (near end of bloom), Purple-stemmed Aster, Calico [Starved] Aster, Spotted Joe-Pye Weed, Sharp-leaved [Mountain, Whorled] Aster, New England Aster (beginning to bloom), Boneset [Thoroughwort] (near end of bloom), Buttercup, Tall [Green-headed] Coneflower, Schreber's Aster, Zigzag [Broad-leaved] Goldenrod

Wolf Pine Trail   *Early Season*: Heart-leaved Aster, Lowrie's Aster, White Snakeroot, Spotted Touch-me-not [Jewelweed] (many in spots), Purple-stemmed Aster (few), White Wood Aster, Goldenrod, Panicled Aster

Late Season: Spotted Touch-me not [Jewelweed], White Snakeroot, Goldenrod (few), Lowrie's Aster (few - beginning to bloom), Heart-leaved Aster (few - beginning to bloom), Purple-stemmed Aster (few), Daisy Fleabane [Sweet Scabious], Helleborine (near end of bloom - one), Small White Aster (one), White Wood Aster (one), White Campion (few)

Trails across from Hancock Shaker Village
See Trail Information for directions.

Road through field *Early Season*: Goldenrod (many), Small White Aster (many), Yarrow [Milfoil], Daisy Fleabane [Sweet Scabious], New England Aster, Common St. Johnswort (near end of bloom), Common Evening Primrose, Purple-stemmed Aster, Spotted Touch-me-not [Jewelweed], Meadowsweet (near end of bloom), Arrow-leaved Tearthumb, Orange Hawkweed [Devil's Paintbrush] (few), Panicled Aster

Late Season: Orange Hawkweed [Devil's Paintbrush] (few), Yarrow [Milfoil], Bladder Campion, Calico [Starved] Aster (few), Small White Aster (few), Daisy Fleabane [Sweet Scabious], Oxeye Daisy (few), Field Hawkweed [King Devil] (one), Wild Carrot [Queen Anne's Lace, Bird's Nest], Yellow Goatsbeard (one), Common Mullein (one), Spotted Joe-Pye Weed, White Snakeroot, Spotted Touch-me-not [Jewelweed], Boneset [Thoroughwort], Purple-stemmed Aster, Lady's Thumb, Maiden Pink , Meadowsweet (near end of bloom), Hairy Willow Herb, Goldenrod (many), Cup Plant [Indian Cup] (many in one place), Common Evening Primrose, New England Aster, Common Comfrey, Purple-flowering Raspberry, Heart-leaved Aster

Road to right through woods *Early Season*: White Wood Aster (many in spots), Lowrie's Aster, Zigzag [Broad-leaved] Goldenrod, Spotted Touch-me-not [Jewelweed] (many in spots), Blue-stemmed [Wreath] Goldenrod, Tall White Lettuce, Tall Nettle, Purple-stemmed Aster, White Snakeroot, Sharp-leaved [Mountain, Whorled] Aster

Late Season: Daisy Fleabane [Sweet Scabious], Goldenrod, White Vervain, Spotted Touch-me-not [Jewelweed] (many), White Wood Aster (many), Spiked Lobelia (near end of bloom), Hog Peanut, Small White Aster, Sharp-leaved [Mountain, Whorled] Aster (quite a few), Tall White Lettuce, White Snakeroot (many in two places), Common Burdock, Tall Nettle, Heart-leaved Aster (beginning to bloom), Blue-stemmed [Wreath] Goldenrod, Zigzag [Broad-leaved] Goldenrod (beginning to bloom), Helleborine (one), Panicled Hawkweed

<u>Road past field toward highway</u>   *Early Season*: Lady's Thumb, Arrow-leaved Tearthumb, Common Burdock, Common Smartweed [Water Pepper], Swamp Smartweed, White Vervain, Beggar Ticks [Sticktight], Calico [Starved] Aster, Heart-leaved Aster, Spotted Touch-me-not [Jewelweed], Panicled Aster, Purple-stemmed Aster

Late Season: Arrow-leaved Tearthumb, Common Burdock, Purple-leaved Willow Herb, Beggar Ticks [Sticktight], Purple-stemmed Aster, Panicled Aster, White Wood Aster, Spotted Touch-me-not [Jewelweed], Common Speedwell, Common St. Johnswort, Goldenrod, Small White Aster, Buttercup (few), Spotted Joe-Pye Weed, Small White Aster, Daisy Fleabane [Sweet Scabious]

<u>Path partway around Shaker reservoir</u> *Early Season*: Small White Aster, Goldenrod, Spotted Joe-Pye Weed, Spotted Touch-me-not [Jewelweed], Wild Mint, Arrow-leaved Tearthumb, Closed [Bottle] Gentian (near end of bloom), Purple-stemmed Aster, Turtlehead

Late Season: Meadowsweet (near end of bloom), Spotted Touch-me-not [Jewelweed], White Wood Aster, Purple-leaved Willow Herb, Calico [Starved] Aster, Goldenrod, Small White Aster, Yarrow [Milfoil], Turtlehead, Spotted Joe-Pye Weed, Wild Mint, Purple-stemmed Aster, Closed [Bottle] Gentian, Silverrod, Black-eyed Susan, Spotted St. Johnswort

LAST TWO WEEKS IN SEPTEMBER

Benedict Pond
See Trail Information for directions.

<u>Path to Pond Loop Trail (beginning at left of swimming area)</u>
Early Season: Heart-leaved Aster, White Wood Aster, Calico [Starved] Aster, Lowrie's Aster, Silverrod (near end of bloom)

Late Season: White Wood Aster, Silverrod (near end of bloom), Goldenrod, Heart-leaved Aster (many), Calico [Starved] Aster, Lowrie's Aster, Small White Aster

<u>Pond Loop Trail to left</u> *(follow blue and white arrows and signs for Pond Loop Trail) Early Season*: Sharp-leaved [Mountain, Whorled] Aster, White Wood Aster (many), Calico [Starved] Aster, Sweet-scented Water Lily (white), Purple-stemmed Aster (many in spots), Goldenrod (near end of bloom), Small White Aster, Panicled Aster, Flat-topped Aster (near end of bloom), Tall White Lettuce, Blue-stemmed [Wreath] Goldenrod, Lowrie's Aster, Heart-leaved Aster, White Snakeroot (few), Swamp Smartweed, Spotted Touch-me-not [Jewelweed] (near end of bloom)

Late Season: White Wood Aster (many), Small White Aster (quite a few eventually), Sharp-leaved [Mountain, Whorled] Aster (quite a few - near end of bloom), Goldenrod (near end of bloom), Purple-stemmed Aster (quite a few), Beggar Ticks [Sticktight], Panicled Aster (few), Flat-topped Aster (near end of bloom), Calico [Starved] Aster (quite a few eventually), Blue-stemmed [Wreath] Goldenrod (many), Pale-leaved Sunflower (near end of bloom), Silverrod, Cattail, Boott's Rattlesnake Root, Sweet-scented Water Lily (white), Zigzag [Broad-leaved] Goldenrod (near end of bloom), Tall White

Lettuce, Lady's Thumb, Heart-leaved Aster, Closed [Bottle] Gentian (few), Panicled Hawkweed (few - near end of bloom), Large-leaved Aster, White Snakeroot (one), Spotted Joe-Pye Weed (near end of bloom), Tall Rattlesnake Root [Gall-of-the-earth], Spotted Touch-me-not [Jewelweed], Daisy Fleabane [Sweet Scabious]

Pleasant Valley

<u>Near entrance</u>   *Late Season:*   Wild Carrot [Queen Anne's Lace, Bird's Nest], Pale-leaved Sunflower, White Snakeroot

<u>Path to Pike's Pond Trail including wildflower garden</u>
See Trail Information for directions.

Early Season: Great Lobelia (near end of bloom), White Snakeroot, Goldenrod, Spiked Lobelia

Late Season: Daisy Fleabane [Sweet Scabious], White Snakeroot, Goldenrod, Pink Turtlehead, Great Lobelia, Spotted Touch-me-not [Jewelweed], Feverfew, Oswego Tea [Bee Balm], Bull Thistle, Heath Aster, White Sweet Clover, Common Evening Primrose, Meadowsweet (near end of bloom), Panicled Aster

<u>Pike's Pond Trail</u>   *Early Season*:   Panicled Aster, Purple-stemmed Aster (many in spots), Goldenrod (near end of bloom), Daisy Fleabane [Sweet Scabious], Calico [Starved] Aster (many), Lowrie's Aster (quite a few), Heart-leaved Aster, Peppermint, Schreber's Aster, White Wood Aster (many in spots), Sharp-leaved [Mountain, Whorled] Aster, Blue-stemmed [Wreath] Goldenrod, (many in spots), Tall White Lettuce, White Snakeroot, Small White Aster

Late Season: White Snakeroot, Goldenrod, Panicled Aster, Spotted Joe-Pye Weed (near end of bloom), Spotted Touch-me-not [Jewelweed], Purple-stemmed Aster, Smaller Forget-me-not, Lowrie's Aster, Daisy Fleabane [Sweet Scabious], Calico [Starved] Aster. Small White Aster, Boneset [Thoroughwort] (near end of bloom), Heart-leaved Aster, Peppermint, White Wood Aster (many), Large-leaved Aster (few), Silverrod (near end of bloom), Schreber's Aster (few), Blue-stemmed [Wreath] Goldenrod, Lion's Foot [Gall-of-the-earth], Boott's Rattlesnake Root

<u>Honeysuckle Lane</u> *See Trail Information for directions.*

Late Season: Spotted Touch-me-not [Jewelweed], Goldenrod, White Snakeroot, Calico [Starved] Aster, Purple-flowering Raspberry (near end of bloom)

<u>Path to Bluebird Trail including wildflower garden</u>
See Trail Information for directions.

Late Season: Daisy Fleabane [Sweet Scabious], White Snakeroot, Goldenrod, Pink Turtlehead, Great Lobelia, Spotted Touch-me-not [Jewelweed], Feverfew, Oswego Tea [Bee Balm], Bull Thistle, Heath Aster, White Sweet Clover, Common Evening Primrose, Meadowsweet (near end of bloom), Panicled Aster, Lady's Thumb, Heart-leaved Aster, Bladder Campion, Oxeye Daisy, Lowrie's Aster, Wild Carrot [Queen Anne's Lace, Bird's Nest]

Bluebird Trail *Early Season*: Goldenrod (near end of bloom)

Late Season: Lowrie's Aster, White Snakeroot, Small White Aster, Goldenrod (many), Calico [Starved] Aster, Panicled Aster, White Wood Aster

Yokun Trail to right *Early Season*: Calico [Starved] Aster (quite a few), White Wood Aster, Zigzag [Broad-leaved] Goldenrod, White Snakeroot, Tall White Lettuce, Heart-leaved Aster, Lowrie's Aster

Late Season: White Wood Aster, White Snakeroot, Tall White Lettuce, Boott's Rattlesnake Root, Silverrod (near end of bloom), Goldenrod (few)

Old Wood Road to left *Early Season*: Some flowers listed on Bluebird and Yokun Trails plus Purple-stemmed Aster, Panicled Aster, Closed [Bottle] Gentian (near end of bloom)

Late Season: Purple-stemmed Aster, Closed [Bottle] Gentian, Lowrie's Aster, Common Cattail

Beaver Lodge Trail to left *Early Season*: No new flowers observed.

Late Season: Purple-stemmed Aster, Calico [Starved] Aster, Blue-stemmed [Wreath] Goldenrod, Small White Aster, Spotted Joe-Pye Weed (near end of bloom), Goldenrod, Buttercup, White Snakeroot (near end of bloom), Boneset [Thoroughwort], Closed [Bottle] Gentian, Smaller Forget-me-not, White Wood Aster

<u>Bluebird Trail to left (twice</u>)   *Early Season*: Beggar Ticks [Sticktight] (near end of bloom)

Late Season: White Wood Aster, Purple-stemmed Aster, Spotted Touch-me-not [Jewelweed]

Arrowhead
See Trail Information for directions to Wildflower Garden.

<u>Wildflower Garden</u> *Early Season*: Panicled Aster, Heart-leaved Aster, Lowrie's Aster, Daisy Fleabane [Sweet Scabious], Goldenrod (near end of bloom), Great Lobelia, Black-eyed Susan, Bladder Campion, White Wood Aster

Late Season: Herb Robert, Goldenrod, Lowrie's Aster, Wild Carrot [Queen Anne's Lace, Bird's Nest], Panicled Aster, Great Lobelia, Pink Turtlehead, Small White Aster, Calico [Starved] Aster

<u>Area to left of Wildflower Garden</u>   *Early Season*: New England Aster, Showy Sunflower (near end of bloom)

Late Season: Wild Carrot [Queen Anne's Lace, Bird's Nest], Lowrie's Aster, Panicled Aster, Showy Sunflower, New England Aster, Daisy Fleabane [Sweet Scabious]

Canoe Meadows

<u>Sacred Way Trail</u>   *See Trail Information for directions.*

Early Season: Panicled Aster (white), Goldenrod (near end of bloom), Purple-stemmed Aster, Arrow-leaved Tearthumb, Larger Bur Marigold, Purple Loosestrife (near end of bloom), Spotted Touch-me-not [Jewelweed], New England Aster, Heart-leaved Aster (many in spots), Lowrie's Aster (many in spots), Zigzag [Broad-leaved] Goldenrod, White Wood Aster, Butter-and-eggs, Panicled Aster (violet tinged), Beggar Ticks [Sticktight] (near end of bloom)

Late Season: Goldenrod (many - some near end of bloom), Panicled Aster (white and light violet-blue - many), Purple-stemmed Aster, Arrow-leaved Tearthumb, Turtlehead, Larger Bur Marigold, Smaller Forget-me-not, Spotted Touch-me-not [Jewelweed], Spotted Joe-Pye Weed (near end of bloom), New England Aster (purple and rose colored), Heart-leaved Aster (quite a few), Lowrie's Aster, Maiden Pink, White Wood Aster (many), Zigzag [Broad-leaved] Goldenrod (quite a few), Calico [Starved] Aster, Bluets [Quaker Ladies, Innocence] (one). Heath Aster (one), Small White Aster, Buttercup, Butter-and-eggs

<u>Road</u>   *See Trail Information for directions.*

Early Season: Goldenrod (near end of bloom), Panicled Aster (white and a few violet tinged), Butter-and-eggs, Tall Nettle, Bladder Campion, White Snakeroot (near end of bloom), Many-flowered Aster (beginning to bloom), Bouncing Bet [Soapwort] (near end of bloom), Spotted Touch-me-not [Jewelweed] (near end of bloom), Lowrie's Aster (many in spots), Heart-leaved Aster (many in spots), White Campion,

Calico [Starved] Aster, Nodding Bur Marigold, Purple-stemmed Aster, Sharp-leaved [Mountain, Whorled] Aster, (near end of bloom), White Wood Aster, New England Aster, Zigzag [Broad-leaved] Goldenrod

Late Season: Panicled Aster (quite a few), Goldenrod (many - some near end of bloom), White Campion (many), Bladder Campion, Common Evening Primrose (near end of bloom), Butter-and-eggs, Spotted Touch-me-not [Jewelweed] (many), Bouncing Bet [Soapwort], Hoary Alyssum, Daisy Fleabane [Sweet Scabious], White Snakeroot, Lowrie's Aster (many), White Wood Aster, Heart-leaved Aster, Cup Plant [Indian Cup] (near end of bloom), Wild Hydrangea (near end of bloom), Small White Aster (quite a few), Calico [Starved] Aster, New England Aster, Purple-stemmed Aster, Sharp-leaved [Mountain, Whorled] Aster, Closed [Bottle] Gentian (few), Spotted Joe-Pye Weed (near end of bloom), Turtlehead (few), Buttercup, Tall [Green-headed] Coneflower (one), Schreber's Aster (near end of bloom), Zigzag [Broad-leaved] Goldenrod

Wolf Pine Trail *Early Season*: Heart-leaved Aster, Lowrie's Aster, Spotted Touch-me-not [Jewelweed] (few- near end of bloom), Goldenrod (few)

Late Season: Heart-leaved Aster, Lowrie's Aster, White Snakeroot, Goldenrod, Spotted Touch-me-not [Jewelweed], Small White Aster, Calico [Starved] Aster, Daisy Fleabane [Sweet Scabious]

Trails across from Hancock Shaker Village
See Trail Information for directions.

Road through field   *Early Season*: Lowrie's Aster, Calico
[Starved] Aster (many), Goldenrod, Spiked Lobelia, Daisy
Fleabane [Sweet Scabious], Small White Aster (few), New
England Aster (quite a few), Bladder Campion (near end of
bloom), Meadowsweet, Purple-stemmed Aster, Common
Evening Primrose, Heart-leaved Aster, Panicled Aster (quite
a few in spots), Yarrow [Milfoil] (near end of bloom)

Late Season: Yarrow [Milfoil], Small White Aster, Calico
[Starved] Aster, Heart-leaved Aster, Goldenrod (quite a few
- near end of bloom), Panicled Aster (white), Wild Carrot
[Queen Anne's Lace, Bird's Nest], Bladder Campion, Daisy
Fleabane [Sweet Scabious], Purple-stemmed Aster, Purple-
flowering Raspberry (near end of bloom), New England Aster,
Meadowsweet (few - near end of bloom), Hollyhock (one),
Common Evening Primrose, Lowrie's Aster

Road to right through woods   *Early Season*: Some flowers
listed in field plus Spotted Touch-me-not [Jewelweed] (quite
a few in spots), White Wood Aster (many in spots), Blue-
stemmed [Wreath] Goldenrod (many in spots), Zigzag [Broad-
leaved] Goldenrod, Tall White Lettuce, Sharp-leaved
[Mountain, Whorled] Aster (near end of bloom), Tall Nettle,
White Snakeroot

Late Season: Panicled Aster, Goldenrod, Daisy Fleabane
[Sweet Scabious], Heart-leaved Aster, Small White Aster,
Calico [Starved] Aster, White Wood Aster (many), Spotted
Touch-me-not [Jewelweed] (near end of bloom), Sharp-leaved
[Mountain, Whorled] Aster, Blue-stemmed [Wreath]
Goldenrod (quite a few), Zigzag [Broad-leaved] Goldenrod,

Boott's Rattlesnake Root, Purple-stemmed Aster, Lowrie's Aster, White Snakeroot (near end of bloom), Arrow-leaved Aster, Tall Rattlesnake Root [Gall-of-the-earth]

Road past field toward highway *Early Season*: Beggar Ticks [Sticktight], Arrow-leaved Tearthumb, Common Smartweed [Water Pepper], Swamp Smartweed, Wavy-leaved Aster

Late Season: Panicled Aster (quite a few), Goldenrod (near end of bloom), White Wood Aster (quite a few), Small White Aster (quite a few), Calico [Starved] Aster, New England Aster, Arrow-leaved Tearthumb, Buttercup, Spotted Joe-Pye Weed, Daisy Fleabane [Sweet Scabious], Spotted Touch-me-not [Jewelweed], Meadowsweet (few), Heart-leaved Aster, Purple-stemmed Aster

Path partway around Shaker reservoir *Early Season*: Some flowers listed before plus Wavy-leaved Aster.

Late Season: Goldenrod, Small White Aster (many), Panicled Aster, Calico [Starved] Aster, Common Evening Primrose, Closed [Bottle] Gentian (many), Meadowsweet (few - near end of bloom), Purple-stemmed Aster, Spotted Touch-me-not [Jewelweed], Lowrie's Aster

FIRST TWO WEEKS IN OCTOBER

Benedict Pond
See Trail Information for directions.

<u>Path to Pond Loop Trail (beginning at left of swimming area)</u>
Early Season: Heart-leaved Aster, Lowrie's Aster

Late Season: White Wood Aster, Heart-leaved Aster, Lowrie's Aster, Calico [Starved] Aster

<u>Pond Loop Trail to left</u>   *Early Season*: *(starting left of swimming area- follow signs for trail and blue and white arrows)* White Wood Aster (near end of bloom), Purple-stemmed Aster (near end of bloom), Calico [Starved] Aster (near end of bloom), Panicled Aster (white - quite a few in spots), Common Cattail, Small White Aster (near end of bloom), Heart-leaved Aster, Lowrie's Aster, Closed [Bottle] Gentian (one), Blue-stemmed [Wreath] Goldenrod , Swamp Smartweed

Late Season: White Wood Aster, Sharp-leaved [Mountain, Whorled] Aster (near end of bloom), Purple-stemmed Aster, Panicled Aster, Large-leaved Aster (lavender and white - near end of bloom), Flat-topped Aster (near end of bloom), Calico [Starved] Aster, Blue-stemmed [Wreath] Goldenrod (near end of bloom), Small White Aster (near end of bloom), Heart-leaved Aster, Lowrie's Aster, Lady's Thumb

Pleasant Valley

<u>Path to Pike's Pond Trail including wildflower garden</u>
See Trail Information for directions.

Early Season: Feverfew, Great Lobelia (near end of bloom), White Snakeroot (near end of bloom), Goldenrod (near end of bloom)

Late Season: Calico [Starved] Aster, Small White Aster, Wild Carrot [Queen Anne's Lace, Bird's Nest], Thin-leaved Sunflower, White Snakeroot, Pink Turtlehead, Goldenrod (near end of bloom), Feverfew, Great Lobelia (near end of bloom), Daisy Fleabane [Sweet Scabious], Bull Thistle, White Sweet Clover (near end of bloom), Black-eyed Susan (near end of bloom), Yarrow [Milfoil]

<u>Pike's Pond Trail</u>   *Early Season*: Small White Aster (near end of bloom), Goldenrod, Panicled Aster (near end of bloom), Purple-stemmed Aster (near end of bloom), Heart-leaved Aster, Lowrie's Aster, Daisy Fleabane [Sweet Scabious] (near end of bloom), Calico [Starved] Aster (near end of bloom), Common Cattail, Schreber's Aster (near end of bloom), White Wood Aster (many), Sharp-leaved [Mountain, Whorled] Aster (near end of bloom), Zigzag [Broad-leaved] Goldenrod (few), Blue-stemmed [Wreath] Goldenrod, White Snakeroot (near end of bloom)

Late Season: Calico [Starved] Aster, Purple-stemmed Aster (near end of bloom), Panicled Aster, Lowrie's Aster, Heart-leaved Aster, White Wood Aster, Blue-stemmed [Wreath] Goldenrod (quite a few), Small White Aster, Cattail, Schreber's Aster, Goldenrod, White Snakeroot (near end of bloom)

<u>Honeysuckle Lane</u>   *See Trail Information for directions.*

Late Season: Daisy Fleabane [Sweet Scabious], White Snakeroot (near end of bloom), Panicled Aster, Goldenrod (near end of bloom), Calico [Starved] Aster

<u>Path to Bluebird Trail including wildflower garden</u>
See Trail Information for directions.

Early Season: Feverfew, Great Lobelia (near end of bloom), White Snakeroot (near end of bloom), Goldenrod (near end of bloom)

Late Season: Wild Carrot [Queen Anne's Lace, Bird's Nest], Thin-leaved Sunflower, White Snakeroot, Pink Turtlehead, Goldenrod (near end of bloom), Feverfew, Great Lobelia (near end of bloom), Daisy Fleabane [Sweet Scabious], Bull Thistle, White Sweet Clover (near end of bloom), Black-eyed Susan (near end of bloom), Yarrow [Milfoil], Lady's Thumb, Wild Radish, Silvery Cinquefoil, Lowrie's Aster, Heart-leaved Aster, Oxeye Daisy, Panicled Aster

<u>Bluebird Trail</u>   *Early Season*: Goldenrod (near end of bloom), Panicled Aster, White Wood Aster

Late Season: Small White Aster, Yarrow [Milfoil], Spiked Lobelia (near end of bloom), White Wood Aster, Goldenrod (few - near end of bloom), Panicled Aster, Meadowsweet (one - near end of bloom)

<u>Yokun Trail to right</u>   *Early Season*: White Wood Aster, Zigzag [Broad-leaved] Goldenrod, Calico [Starved] Aster, Common Cattail, Lowrie's Aster, Daisy Fleabane [Sweet Scabious], Heart-leaved Aster, Blue-stemmed [Wreath] Goldenrod

Late Season: White Wood Aster, Calico [Starved] Aster, Small White Aster, Lowrie's Aster, Heart-leaved Aster, Silverrod (near end of bloom), Blue-stemmed [Wreath] Goldenrod

<u>Old Wood Road to left</u>   *Early Season*: Small White Aster

Late Season: Tall White Lettuce, Closed [Bottle] Gentian (near end of bloom), Cattail

<u>Beaver Lodge Trail to left</u>   *Early Season*: Purple-stemmed Aster (near end of bloom), Panicled Aster

Late Season: Small White Aster, Goldenrod, Purple-stemmed Aster, Calico [Starved] Aster, Buttercup, White Wood Aster

<u>Bluebird Trail to left (twice*)*   *Early and Late Seasons*: No flowers were observed.

Arrowhead
See Trail Information for directions to Wildflower Garden.

<u>Wildflower Garden</u>   *Early Season*: Wild Carrot [Queen Anne's Lace, Bird's Nest], Heart-leaved Aster (near end of bloom), Lowrie's Aster (near end of bloom), White Wood Aster, Black-eyed Susan, Panicled Aster (few)

Late Season: Heart-leaved Aster, Lowrie's Aster (some near end of bloom), Great Lobelia (near end of bloom), Goldenrod (near end of bloom), Daisy Fleabane [Sweet Scabious], Closed [Bottle] Gentian, Panicled Aster (white), Wild Carrot [Queen Anne's Lace, Bird's Nest]

Area to left of Wildflower Garden   *Early Season*: New England Aster (near end of bloom)

Late Season: Panicled Aster (white), New England Aster

Canoe Meadows

Sacred Way Trail   *See Trail Information for directions.*

Early Season: Panicled Aster (mostly white, some violet-tinged - many near end of bloom), New England Aster (near end of bloom), Heart-leaved Aster (near end of bloom), Lowrie's Aster (near end of bloom), White Wood Aster, Purple-stemmed Aster (near end of bloom)

Late Season: *Beginning area recently mowed.*
Panicled Aster (white and violet tinged), Goldenrod (near end of bloom), New England Aster (near end of bloom), Heart-leaved Aster (quite a few), Pearly Everlasting , Lowrie's Aster (few), White Wood Aster (near end of bloom), Calico [Starved] Aster, Small White Aster (near end of bloom), Buttercup (one), Purple-stemmed Aster

<u>Road</u>   *See Trail Information for directions.*

Early Season: Goldenrod (near end of bloom), Many-flowered Aster, Panicled Aster (near end of bloom), Tall Nettle, Bouncing Bet [Soapwort] (near end of bloom), Heart-leaved Aster (quite a few), Lowrie's Aster (near end of bloom), Daisy Fleabane [Sweet Scabious], Sharp-leaved [Mountain, Whorled] Aster (near end of bloom), Calico [Starved] Aster, White Wood Aster, New England Aster (near end of bloom)

Late Season: Some of beginning area recently mowed.
Panicled Aster (white and violet-tinged), Butter-and-eggs (few), Goldenrod (few - near end of bloom), Bouncing Bet [Soapwort] (few - near end of bloom), Heart-leaved Aster, Lowrie's Aster, Daisy Fleabane [Sweet Scabious], Blue-stemmed [Wreath] Goldenrod, New England Aster, Cattail, White Wood Aster (near end of bloom), White Snakeroot (one), Small White Aster (one)

<u>Wolf Pine Trail</u>   *Early Season*: Lowrie's Aster (near end of bloom), Heart-leaved Aster (near end of bloom), Purple-stemmed Aster (near end of bloom), Daisy Fleabane [Sweet Scabious], White Wood Aster

Late Season: Lowrie's Aster, Heart-leaved Aster, Calico [Starved] Aster (few), Small White Aster (few)

Trails across from Hancock Shaker Village
See Trail Information for directions.

Road through field   *Early Season*: Daisy Fleabane [Sweet Scabious], Wild Radish, Yarrow [Milfoil], New England Aster, Small White Aster, Rush Aster, Calico [Starved] Aster, Panicled Aster

Late Season (much of this mowed): Calico [Starved] Aster (near end of bloom), Small White Aster, Panicled Aster (white), Daisy Fleabane [Sweet Scabious]. Maiden Pink, Lowrie's Aster, Goldenrod (near end of bloom), New England Aster, Wild Carrot [Queen Anne's Lace, Bird's Nest], Purple-stemmed Aster, Heart-leaved Aster

Road to right through woods   *Early Season*: White Wood Aster, Heart-leaved Aster (near end of bloom)

Late Season: Panicled Aster, Goldenrod (near end of bloom), Small White Aster, Heart-leaved Aster, Calico [Starved] Aster, White Wood Aster (near end of bloom), Blue-stemmed [Wreath] Goldenrod, Purple-stemmed Aster, Tall Rattlesnake Root [Gall-of-the-earth]

Road past field toward highway   *Early Season*: White Wood Aster, Panicled Aster, Small White Aster, Heart-leaved Aster, Purple-stemmed Aster, Daisy Fleabane [Sweet Scabious]

Late Season: Panicled Aster, White Wood Aster (near end of bloom), Heart-leaved Aster, Calico [Starved] Aster, Small White Aster, Lowrie's Aster, New England Aster, Buttercup (one), Daisy Fleabane [Sweet Scabious]

<u>Path partway around Shaker reservoir</u> *Early Season*: Small White Aster, Goldenrod (near end of bloom), Lowrie's Aster, Panicled Aster, Closed [Bottle] Gentian, Purple-stemmed Aster

Late Season: Small White Aster (near end of bloom), Goldenrod (near end of bloom), Panicled Aster, Meadowsweet (one - near end of bloom), Closed [Bottle] Gentian (near end of bloom)

LAST TWO WEEKS IN OCTOBER

Benedict Pond
See Trail Information for directions.

<u>Path to Pond Loop Trail (beginning at left of swimming area)</u>
Early Season: Lowrie's Aster (few), Arrow-leaved Aster, Heart-leaved Aster (near end of bloom)

Late Season: Lowrie's Aster, Heart-leaved Aster, White Wood Aster

<u>Pond Loop Trail to left</u> *Early Season*: White Wood Aster , Purple-stemmed Aster, Heart-leaved Aster (few), Lowrie's Aster (one), Panicled Aster (all near end of bloom)

Late Season: White Wood Aster, Blue-stemmed [Wreath] Goldenrod (near end of bloom), Closed [Bottle] Gentian (one), Lowrie's Aster, Calico [Starved] Aster (near end of bloom), Swamp Smartweed

Pleasant Valley

<u>Path to Pike's Pond Trail including wildflower garden.</u>
See Trail Information for directions.

Early Season: Feverfew, Lowrie's Aster, Panicled Aster, Calico [Starved] Aster, Goldenrod, White Snakeroot

Late Season: Goldenrod (near end of bloom), Daisy Fleabane [Sweet Scabious] (near end of bloom), Feverfew, White Sweet Clover (near end of bloom)

<u>Pike's Pond Trail</u>   *Early Season*: Lowrie's Aster, Common Cattail, Daisy Fleabane [Sweet Scabious], Schreber's Aster, White Wood Aster, Purple-stemmed Aster, Panicled Aster, White Snakeroot, Goldenrod (all near end of bloom)

Late Season: Cattail, Daisy Fleabane [Sweet Scabious], Calico [Starved] Aster (two), Lowrie's Aster (two), Heart-leaved Aster (one), Schreber's Aster (one), Purple-stemmed Aster, White Wood Aster (all near end of bloom)

<u>Honeysuckle Lane</u>   *See Trail Information for directions.*

Late Season: No flowers were observed.

<u>Path to Bluebird Trail including wildflower garden</u>
See Trail Information for directions.

Early Season: Feverfew, Lowrie's Aster, Panicled Aster, Calico [Starved] Aster, Goldenrod, White Snakeroot.

Late Season: Goldenrod, Daisy Fleabane [Sweet Scabious], Feverfew, White Sweet Clover (all near end of bloom)

<u>Bluebird Trail</u>   *Early and Late Seasons*: No flowers were observed.

<u>Yokun Trail to right</u>   *Early Season*: White Wood Aster, Heart-leaved Aster, Calico [Starved] Aster (all near end of bloom)

Late Season: Heart-leaved Aster (few), Blue-stemmed [Wreath] Goldenrod (near end of bloom), White Wood Aster (near end of bloom), Lowrie's Aster (few), Silverrod (most near end of bloom)

<u>Old Wood Road to left</u>   *Early Season*: No flowers were observed.

Late Season: Panicled Aster

<u>Beaver Lodge Trail to left</u> *Early Season*: Common Cattail, White Wood Aster (near end of bloom)

Late Season: Small White Aster (two)

<u>Bluebird Trail to left (twice)</u>   *Early Season*: No flowers were observed.

Late Season: White Wood Aster (near end of bloom)

Arrowhead
See Trail Information for directions to Wildflower Garden.

<u>Wildflower Garden</u>   *Early Season*: Lowrie's Aster, Wild Carrot [Queen Anne's Lace, Bird's Nest] (near end of bloom), Daisy Fleabane [Sweet Scabious] (near end of bloom), White Wood Aster (near end of bloom)

Late Season: Heart-leaved Aster (few), Daisy Fleabane [Sweet Scabious], Goldenrod (near end of bloom)

Canoe Meadows

<u>Sacred Way Trail</u>   *See Trail Information for directions.*

Early Season: Goldenrod, Panicled Aster, Pearly Everlasting (all near end of bloom)

Late Season: Panicled Aster (white and a few lilac-tinged - near end of bloom), Goldenrod (few - near end of bloom), Heart-leaved Aster (few - near end of bloom), Arrow-leaved Aster (one white - near end of bloom), Heart-leaved Aster (few - near end of bloom), Purple-stemmed Aster (one - near end of bloom)

<u>Road</u>   *See Trail Information for directions.*

Early Season: Goldenrod (looks good where it has been mowed; other places near end of bloom), Tall Nettle, Panicled Aster (near end of bloom), Heart-leaved Aster (near end of bloom), Daisy Fleabane [Sweet Scabious]

Late Season: Panicled Aster (white and lilac tinged), Goldenrod, Daisy Fleabane [Sweet Scabious], Heart-leaved Aster, White Campion, Cattail, Small White Aster (all few and near end of bloom)

<u>Wolf Pine Trail</u>   *Early Season*: Heart-leaved Aster (few - near end of bloom)

Late Season: Heart-leaved Aster, Calico Aster (both few and near end of bloom)

Trails across from Hancock Shaker Village
See Trail Information for directions.

<u>Road through field</u> *Early Season*: Yarrow [Milfoil], Daisy Fleabane [Sweet Scabious] (one - near end of bloom), Calico [Starved] Aster (one - near end of bloom), Heart-leaved Aster (few - near end of bloom), Goldenrod (few - near end of bloom), Lowrie's Aster (few), Arrow-leaved Aster (few), Panicled Aster (few - near end of bloom)

Late Season: Heart-leaved Aster (near end of bloom), Calico [Starved] Aster, Yarrow [Milfoil] (near end of bloom), Panicled Aster (white), Goldenrod (looks good in mowed areas; in other places near end of bloom), Arrow-leaved Aster

<u>Road to right through woods</u> *Early Season*: White Wood Aster, Arrow-leaved Aster, Schreber's Aster

Late Season: White Wood Aster, Daisy Fleabane [Sweet Scabious] (near end of bloom)

<u>Road past field toward highway</u> *Early Season*: Panicled Aster

Late Season: Panicled Aster, Calico [Starved] Aster, Small White Aster, Daisy Fleabane [Sweet Scabious] (all - few and near end of bloom*)*

<u>Path partway around Shaker reservoir</u>   *Early Season:*
Panicled Aster, Golden Alexanders, Goldenrod, Calico
[Starved] Aster, Small White Aster, Meadowsweet, Zigzag
[Broad-leaved] Goldenrod, Lowrie's Aster (all - few and near
end of bloom)

Late Season: Yarrow [Milfoil], Closed [Bottle] Gentian (near
end of bloom), Lowrie's Aster

SCIENTIFIC-COMMON NAME EQUIVALENTS

Achillea millefolium - Milfoil
Achillea millefolium - Yarrow
Aconitum uncinatum - Monkshood, Wild
Actaea - Baneberry
Actaea pachypoda - Baneberry, White
Actaea pachypoda - Doll's Eyes
Actaea rubra - Baneberry, Red
Agrimonia gryposepala - Agrimony
Ajuga reptans - Bugle
Alcea rosea - Hollyhock
Alliaria officinalis - Mustard, Garlic
Allium tricoccum - Leek, Wild
Allium tricoccum - Ramps
Amelanchier arborea - Shadbush, Common
Amelanchier laevis - Shadbush, Smooth
Amphicarpa bracteata - Hog Peanut
Anaphalis margaritacea - Everlasting, Pearly
Anemone canadensis - Anemone, Canada
Anemone quinquefolia - Anemone, Wood
Anemone quinquefolia - Windflower
Anemone virginiana - Anemone, Tall
Anemone virginiana - Thimbleweed
Anemonella thalictroides - Anemone, Rue
Angelica atropurpurea - Angelica, Great
Antennaria canadensis - Pussytoes, Canada
Antennaria neglecta - Pussytoes, Field
Apocynum cannabinum - Hemp, Indian
Apocynun androsa emifolium - Dogbane, Spreading
Aquilegia canadensis - Columbine, Wild
Aquilegia vulgaris - Columbine, European
Aquilegia vulgaris - Columbine, Garden

Aralia nudicaulis - Sarsaparilla, Wild
Arctium minus - Burdock, Common
Arenaria lateriflora - Sandwort, Blunt-leaved
Arenaria lateriflora - Sandwort, Grove
Arisaema - Jack-in-the-pulpit
Arisaema atrorubens - Indian Turnip
Asarum canadense - Ginger, Wild
Asclepias incarnata - Milkweed, Swamp
Asclepias syriaca - Milkweed, Common
Asperula odorata - Woodruff
Aster acuminatus - Aster, Mountain
Aster acuminatus - Aster, Sharp-leaved
Aster acuminatus - Aster, Whorled
Aster cordifolius - Aster, Heart-leaved
Aster divaricatus - Aster, White Wood
Aster ericoides - Aster, Many-flowered
Aster junciformis - Aster, Rush
Aster laevis - Aster, Smooth
Aster lateriflorus - Aster, Calico
Aster lateriflorus - Aster, Starved
Aster lowrieanus - Aster, Lowrie's
Aster macrophyllus - Aster, Large-leaved
Aster novae-angliae - Aster, New England
Aster pilosus - Aster, Heath
Aster puniceus - Aster, Purple-stemmed
Aster sagittifolius - Aster, Arrow-leaved
Aster schreberi - Aster, Schreber's
Aster simplex - Aster, Panicled
Aster umbellatus - Aster, Flat-topped
Aster undulatus - Aster, Wavy-leaved
Aster vimineus - Aster, Small White
Astilbe - Astilbe
Barbarea vulgaris - Rocket, Yellow
Barbarea vulgaris - Winter Cress, Common

Berberis thunbergii - Barberry, Japanese
Berteroa incana - Alyssum, Hoary
Bidens cernua - Bur Marigold, Nodding
Bidens frondosa - Beggar Ticks
Bidens frondosa - Sticktight
Bidens laevis - Bur Marigold, Larger
Caltha palustris - Cowslip
Caltha palustris - Marigold, Marsh
Campanula repunculoides - Bellflower, Creeping
Capsella bursa-pastoris - Shepherd's Purse
Cardamine pratenses - Cuckooflower
Cardamine pratenses - Lady's Smock
Caulophyllum thalictroides - Cohosh, Blue
Celastrus - Bittersweet, Asiatic
Centaurea maculosa - Knapweed, Spotted
Centaurium umbellatum - Centaury
Cephalanthus occidentalis - Buttonbush
Cerastium arvense - Chickweed, Field
Chaenomeles speciosa - Quince, Flowering
Chelidonium majus - Celandine
Chelone glabra - Turtlehead
Chelone lyoni - Turtlehead, Pink
Chrysanthemum leucanthemum - Daisy, Oxeye
Chrysanthemum parthenium - Feverfew
Cichorium intybus - Chicory
Cimicifuga racemosa - Cohosh, Black
Cimicifuga racemosa - Snakeroot, Black
Circaea quadrisulcata - Nightshade, Enchanter's
Cirsium arvense - Thistle, Canada
Cirsium vulgare - Thistle, Bull
Claytonia caroliniana - Spring Beauty, Carolina
Clematis virginiana - Virgin's Bower
Clintonia borealis - Bluebead

Clintonia borealis - Clintonia, Yellow
Collinsonia canadensis - Horse Balm
Collinsonia canadensis - Richweed
Collinsonia canadensis - Stoneroot
Convallaria majalis - Lily-of-the-valley
Convolvulus sepium - Bindweed, Hedge
Coptis groenlandica - Goldenthread
Cornus amomum - Dogwood, Silky
Cornus canadensis - Bunchberry
Cornus canadensis - Cornel, Dwarf
Cornus obliqua - Dogwood, Pale
Cornus racemosa - Dogwood, Gray
Cornus racemosa - Dogwood, Panicled
Cornus rugosa - Dogwood, Round-leaved
Cornus Solonifera - Dogwood, Red-osier
Crataegus - Hawthorn
Cypripedium acaule - Lady's Slipper, Pink
Cypripedium acaule - Moccasin Flower
Cypripedium calceolus pubescens - Lady's Slipper, Larger
Yellow
Daphne mezereon -Daphne, February
Daucus carota - Bird's Nest
Daucus carota - Carrot, Wild
Daucus carota - Queen Anne's Lace
Dentaria diphylla - Crinkleroot
Dentaria diphylla - Toothwort
Desmodium glutinosum - Tick Trefoil, Pointed-leaved
Dianthus deltoides - Pink, Maiden
Dicentra - Dutchman's Breeches
Dicentra spectabilis - Bleeding Heart
Diervilla lonicera - Honeysuckle, Bush
Dodecatheon meadia - Shooting Star
Echinacea purpurea - Coneflower, Purple
Echinocystis lobata - Balsam Apple, Wild

Echinocystis lobata - Cucumber, Wild
Epigaea regens - Arbutus, Trailing
Epigaea repens - Mayflower
Epilobium coloratum - Willow Herb, Purple-leaved
Epilobium glandulosum - Willow Herb, Northern
Epilobium hirsutum - Willow Herb, Hairy
Epipactis helleborine - Helleborine
Erigeron annuus - Fleabane, Daisy
Erigeron annuus - Scabious, Sweet
Erigeron philadelphicus - Fleabane, Common
Erigeron philadelphicus - Fleabane, Philadelphia
Erigeron pulchellus - Plantain, Robin's
Erigeron strigosus - Fleabane, Lesser Daisy
Erthronium americanum - Adder's Tongue, Yellow
Erthronium americanum - Lily, Trout
Eupatorium aromaticum - Snakeroot, Smaller White
Eupatorium maculatum - Joe-Pye Weed, Spotted
Eupatorium perfoliatum - Boneset
upatorium perfoliatum - Thoroughwort
Eupatorium rugosum - Snakeroot, White
Forsythia - Forsythia
Fragaria - Strawberry
Fragaria vesca - Strawberry, Wood
Fragaria Virginiana - Strawberry, Wild
Galanthus nivalis - Snowdrop
Galanthus nivalis - Snowdrop, Early
Galium asprellum - Bedstraw, Rough
Galium trifidum - Bedstraw, Small
Gaultheria procumbens - Checkerberry
Gaultheria procumbens - Wintergreen
Gaylussacia dumosa - Huckleberry, Dwarf
Gentiana clausa - Gentian, Bottle
Gentiana clausa - Gentian, Closed
Geranium maculatum - Cranesbill, Spotted

Geranium maculatum - Geranium, Wild
Geranium robertianum - Herb Robert
Geum aleppicum - Avens, Yellow
Geum canadense - Avens, White
Geum virginianum - Avens, Cream-colored
Glechoma hederacea - Gill-over-the-ground
Glechoma hederacea - Ivy, Ground
Gnaphalium obtusifolium - Catfoot
Gnaphalium obtusifolium - Everlasting, Sweet
Helianthus decapetalus - Sunflower, Thin-leaved
Helianthus laetiflorus - Sunflower, Showy
Helianthus strumosus - Sunflower, Pale-leaved
Hemerocallis Fulva - Lily, Day
Hepatica acutiloba - Hepatica, Sharp-lobed
Hesperis matronalis - Rocket, Dame's
Hesperis matronalis - Violet, Dame's
Heterotheca subaxillaris - Camphorweed
Hieracium aurantiacum - Devil's Paintbrush
Hieracium aurantiacum - Hawkweed, Orange
Hieracium paniculatum - Hawkweed, Panicled
Hieracium pilosella - Mouse Ear
Hieracium pratense - Hawkweed, Field
Hieracium pratense - King Devil
Hieracium venosum - Rattlesnake Weed
Houstonia caerulea - Bluets
Houstonia caerulea - Innocence
Houstonia caerulea - Quaker Ladies
Hydrangea arborescens - Hydrangea, Wild
Hydrophyllum virginianum - Waterleaf, Virginia
Hypericum perforatum - St. Johnswort, Common
Hypericum punctatum - St. Johnswort, Spotted
Hypericum virginicum - St. Johnswort, Marsh
Hypochoeris radicata - Cat's Ear
Impatiens capensis - Jewelweed

Impatiens capensis - Touch-me-not, Spotted
Iris cristata - Iris, Crested
Iris pseudacorus - Iris, Yellow
Iris sibirica - Iris, Siberian
Iris verna - Iris, Dwarf
Iris verna - Iris, Vernal
Iris versicolor - Iris, Larger Blue Flag
Kalmia latifolia - Laurel, Mountain
Laportea canadensis - Nettle, Wood
Lapsana communis - Nipplewort
Leonurus cardiaca - Motherwort
Ligustrum vulgare - Privet
Lilium canadense - Lily, Canada
Lilium canadense - Lily, Meadow
Lilium canadense - Lily, Wild Yellow
Lilium superbum - Lily, Turk's-cap
Linaria vulgaris - Butter-and-eggs
Lobelia siphilitica - Lobelia, Great
Lobelia spicata - Lobelia, Spiked
Lonicera bella - Honeysuckle, Hybrid of Morrow's and Tartarian
Lonicera morrowi - Honeysuckle, Morrow's
Lonicera tatarica - Honeysuckle, Tartarian
Lotus corniculatus - Trefoil, Birdsfoot
Lupinus polyphyllus - Lupine, Garden
Lychnis alba - Campion, White
Lychnis flos-cuculi - Cuckooflower
Lychnis flos-cuculi - Ragged Robin
Lycopus americanus - Horehound, Water
Lycopus unifloris - Bugleweed, Northern
Lycopus virginicus - Bugleweed, Virginia
Lyonia ligustrina - Maleberry
Lysimachia ciliata - Loosestrife, Fringed
Lysimachia nummularia - Moneywort

Lysimachia quadrifolia - Loosestrife, Four-leaved
Lysimachia quadrifolia - Loosestrife, Whorled
Lysimachia terrestris - Loosestrife, Yellow
Lysimachia terrestris - Swamp Candles
Lysimachia vulgaris - Loosestrife, Garden
Lythrum salicaria - Loosestrife, Purple
Maianthemum canadense - Lily-of-the-valley, Wild
Maianthemum canadense - Mayflower, Canada
Malus - Apple
Malus - Crab Apple
Malva moschata - Mallow, Musk
Medeola virginiana - Cucumber Root, Indian
Medicago sativa - Alfalfa
Medicago sativa - Lucerne
Melampyrum lineare - Cowwheat
Melilotus alba - Clover, White Sweet
Mentha arvensis - Mint, Wild
Mentha piperita - Peppermint
Mertensia virginica - Bluebells, Virginia
Mertensia virginica - Cowslip, Virginia
Mitella diphylla - Bishop's Cap
Mitella diphylla - Miterwort
Monarda didyma - Bee Balm
Monarda didyma - Oswego Tea
Monarda fistulosa - Bergamot, Wild
Monarda media - Bergamot, Purple
Monotropa hypopithys - Beechdrops, False
Monotropa hypopithys - Pinesap
Monotropa uniflora - Corpse Plant
Monotropa uniflora - Indian Pipe
Myosotis laxa - Forget-me-not, Smaller
Narcissus - Daffodil
Nasturtium officinale - Watercress
Nuphar variegatum - Lily, Cow

Nuphar variegatum - Lily, Yellow Pond
Nuphar variegatum - Spatterdock
Nymphaea odorata - Lily, Sweet-scented Water
Oenothera biennis - Evening Primrose, Common
Oenothera fruticosa - Sundrops
Oenothera perennis - Sundrops, Small
Orobanche uniflora - Cancerroot, One-flowered
Orobanche uniflora - Ghost Pipe
Osmorhiza longistylis - Aniseroot
Oxalis europaea - Sorrel, Yellow Wood
Oxalis montana - Sorrel, Common Wood
Pachysandra terminalis - Spurge, Japanese
Panax trifolius - Ginseng, Dwarf
Pastinaca sativa - Parsnip, Wild
Pedicularis canadensis - Betony, Wood
Pedicularis canadensis - Lousewort
Phlox divaricata - Phlox, Wild Blue
Phytolacca americana - Pokeweed
Podophyllum peltatum - Mandrake
Podophyllum peltatum - Mayapple
Polemonium reptans - Varerian, Greek
Polemonium van-bruntiae - Jacob's Ladder
Polygonatum canaliculatum - Solomon's Seal, Great
Polygonatum pubescens - Solomon's Seal, Hairy
Polygonum coccineum - Smartweed, Swamp
Polygonum hydropiper - Smartweed, Common
Polygonum hydropiper - Water Pepper
Polygonum lapathifolium - Smartweed, Dock-leaved
Polygonum lapathifolium - Smartweed, Nodding
Polygonum lapathifolium - Smartweed, Pale
Polygonum pensylvanicum - Knotweed, Pink
Polygonum pensylvanicum - Pinkweed
Polygonum persicaria - Lady's Thumb
Polygonum sagittatum - Tearthumb, Arrow-leaved

Potentilla argentea - Cinquefoil, Silvery
Potentilla canadensis - Cinquefoil, Dwarf
Potentilla norvegica - Cinquefoil, Rough
Potentilla recta - Cinquefoil, Rough-fruited
Potentilla recta - Cinquefoil, Sulphur
Potentilla simplex - Cinquefoil, Common
Prenanthes - Rattlesnake Root
Prenanthes alba - Lettuce, White
Prenanthes altissima - Lettuce, Tall White
Prenanthes boottii - Rattlesnake Root, Boott's
Prenanthes trifoliata - Gall-of-the-earth
Prenanthes trifoliata - Lion's Foot
Prenanthes trifoliata - Rattlesnake Root, Tall
Primula laurentiana - Primrose, Bird's-eye
Primula polyantha - Primrose, Polyanthus
Prunella vulgaris - Heal-all
Prunella vulgaris - Selfheal
Prunus pensylvanica - Cherry, Bird
Prunus pensylvanica - Cherry, Fire
Prunus pensylvanica - Cherry, Pin
Prunus virginiena - Chokecherry
Pycnanthemum tenuifolium - Mountain Mint, Narrow-
leaved
Pyrola elliptica - Shinleaf
Pyrus - Chokeberry
Pyrus melanocarpa - Chokeberry, Black
Ranunculus - Buttercup
Ranunculus abortivus - Crowfoot, Small-flowered
Ranunculus sceleratus - Crowfoot, Cursed
Raphanus raphanistrum - Radish, Wild
Ratibida pinnata - Coneflower, Gray-headed
Rhododendron - Rhododendron
Rhododendron nudiflorum - Azalea, Pink
Rhododendron nudiflorum - Pinxter Flower

Rhus radicans - Ivy, Poison
Ribes sativum - Currant, Garden
Rosa blanda - Rose, Smooth
Rosa multiflora - Rose, Multiflora
Rosa rugosa - Rose, Rugosa
Rubus allegheniensis - Blackberry, Common
Rubus flagellaris - Dewberry
Rubus hispidus - Dewberry, Swamp
Rubus occidentalis - Raspberry, Black
Rubus occidentalis - Thimbleberry
Rubus odoratus - Raspberry, Purple-flowering
Rudbeckia laciniata - Coneflower, Green-headed
Rudbeckia laciniata - Coneflower, Tall
Rudbeckia serotina - Black-eyed Susan
Sagittaria latifolia - Arrowhead, Common
Sambucus canadensis - Elder, Common
Sambucus pubens - Elder, Red-berried
Sanguinaria canadensis - Bloodroot
Saponaria officinalis - Bouncing Bet
Saponaria officinalis - Soapwort
Satureja vulgaris - Basil, Wild
Scilla sibirica - Scilla, Siberian
Scilla sibirica - Squill, Spring
Scutellaria epilobifolia - Skullcap, Marsh
Scutellaria lateriflora - Skullcap, Mad-dog
Senecio aureus - Ragwort, Golden
Senecio obovatus - Ragwort, Round-leaved
Silene cucubalus - Campion, Bladder
Silphium perfoliatum - Cup Plant
Silphium perfoliatum - Indian Cup
Sisymbrium officinale - Mustard, Hedge
Sisyrinchium - Blue-eyed Grass
Smilacina racemosa - Solomon's Seal, False
Smilacina racemosa - Spikenard, Wild

Solanum dulcamara - Nightshade, Bittersweet
Solidago - Goldenrod
Solidago bicolor - Silverrod
Solidago caesia - Goldenrod, Blue-stemmed
Solidago caesia - Goldenrod, Wreath
Solidago flexicaulis - Goldenrod, Broad-leaved
Solidago flexicaulis - Goldenrod, Zigzag
Spiraea - Spiraea
Spiraea alba - Meadowsweet, Narrow-leaved
Spiraea latifolia - Meadowsweet
Spiraea tomentosa - Hardhack
Spiraea tomentosa - Steeplebush
Stellaria graminea - Stitchwort, Lesser
Streptopus roseus - Mandarin, Rose
Streptopus roseus - Rosybells
Streptopus roseus - Twisted Stalk, Rose
Symphytum officinale - Comfrey, Common
Symplocarpus foetidus - Skunk Cabbage
Syringa - Lilac
Tanacetum vulgare - Tansy
Taraxacum - Dandelions
Thalictrum dioicum - Meadow Rue, Early
Thalictrum Polygamum - Meadow Rue, Tall
Tiarella cordifolia - Foamflower
Tiarella cordifolia - Miterwort, False
Tragopogon pratensis - Goatsbeard, Yellow
Trichostema dichotomum - Blue Curls
Trientalis Boealis - Starflower
Trillium cernuum - Trillium, Nodding
Trillium erectum - Birthroot
Trillium erectum - Trillium, Purple
Trillium erectum - Trillium, Red
Trillium erectum - Wake-robin
Trillium grandiflorum - Trillium, Large-flowered

Trillium sessile - Toadshade
Trillium sessile - Trillium, Toad
Trillium undulatum - Trillium, Painted
Tussilago farfara - Coltsfoot
Typha - Cattail
Typha angustifolia - Cattail, Narrow-leaved
Typha latifolia - Cattail, Common
Urtica procera - Nettle, Tall
Uvularia perfoliata - Bellwort
Uvularia sessilifolia - Bellwort, Sessile-leaved
Uvularia sessilifolia - Wild Oats
Vaccinium angustifolium - Blueberry, Early Low
Vaccinium corymbosum - Blueberry, Highbush
Vaccinium corymbosum - Blueberry, Swamp
Valeriana officinalis - Heliotrope, Garden
Vareriana officinalis - Valerian, Garden
Veratrum viride - Hellebore, False
Veratrum viride - Hellebore, White
Veratrum viride - Poke, Indian
Verbascum thapsus - Mullein, Common
Verbena hastata - Vervain, Blue
Verbena urticifolia - Vervain, White
Veronica chamaedrys - Speedwell, Bird's-eye
Veronica chamaedrys - Speedwell, Germander
Veronica officinalis - Speedwell, Common
Viburnum acerifolium - Dockmackie
Viburnum acerifolium - Viburnum, Maple-leaved
Viburnum alnifolium - Hobblebush
Viburnum lentago - Nannyberry
Viburnum lentago - Vibernum, Sweet
Viburnum recognitum - Arrowwood
Viburnum trilobum - Cranberry, Highbush
Vicia cracca - Vetch, Cow
Vicia cracca - Vetch, Tufted

Vinca minor - Myrtle
Viola - Violet
Viola Kitaibeliana - Pansy, Field
Zizia aurea - Alexanders, Golden

COMMON-SCIENTIFIC NAME EQUIVALENTS

Adder's Tongue, Yellow - *Erthronium americanum*
Agrimony - *Agrimonia gryposepala*
Alexanders, Golden - *Zizia aurea*
Alfalfa - *Medicago sativa*
Alyssum, Hoary - *Berteroa incana*
Anemone, Canada - *Anemone canadensis*
Anemone, Rue - *Anemonella thalictroides*
Anemone, Tall - *Anemone virginiana*
Anemone, Wood - *Anemone quinquefolia*
Angelica, Great - *Angelica atropurpurea*
Aniseroot - *Osmorhiza longistylis*
Apple - *Malus*
Arbutus, Trailing - *Epigaea regens*
Arrowhead, Common - *Sagittaria latifolia*
Arrowwood - *Viburnum recognitum*
Aster, Arrow-leaved - *Aster sagittifolius*
Aster, Calico - *Aster lateriflorus*
Aster, Flat-topped - *Aster umbellatus*
Aster, Heart-leaved - *Aster cordifolius*
Aster, Heath - *Aster pilosus*
Aster, Large-leaved - *Aster macrophyllus*
Aster, Lowrie's - *Aster lowrieanus*
Aster, Many-flowered - *Aster ericoides*
Aster, Mountain - *Aster acuminatus*
Aster, New England - *Aster novae-angliae*
Aster, Panicled - *Aster simplex*
Aster, Purple-stemmed - *Aster puniceus*
Aster, Rush - *Aster junciformis*
Aster, Schreber's - *Aster schreberi*
Aster, Sharp-leaved - *Aster acuminatus*
Aster, Small White - *Aster vimineus*
Aster, Smooth - *Aster laevis*

Aster, Starved - *Aster lateriflorus*
Aster, Wavy-leaved- *Aster undulatus*
Aster, White Wood - *Aster divaricatus*
Aster, Whorled - *Aster acuminatus*
Astilbe - *Astilbe*
Avens, Cream-colored - *Geum virginianum*
Avens, White - *Geum canadense*
Avens, Yellow - *Geum aleppicum*
Azalea, Pink - *Rhododendron nudiflorum*
Balsam Apple, Wild - *Echinocystis lobata*
Baneberry - *Actaea*
Baneberry, Red - *Actaea rubra*
Baneberry, White - *Actaea pachypoda*
Barberry, Japanese - *Berberis thunbergii*
Basil, Wild - *Satureja vulgaris*
Bedstraw, Rough - *Galium asprellum*
Bedstraw, Small - *Galium trifidum*
Bee Balm - *Monarda didyma*
Beechdrops, False - *Monotropa hypopithys*
Beggar Ticks - *Bidens frondosa*
Bellflower, Creeping - *Campanula repunculoides*
Bellwort - *Uvularia perfoliata*
Bellwort, Sessile-leaved - *Uvularia sessilifolia*
Bergamot, Purple - *Monarda media*
Bergamot, Wild - *Monarda fistulosa*
Betony, Wood - *Pedicularis canadensis*
Bindweed, Hedge - *Convolvulus sepium*
Bird's Nest - *Daucus carota*
Birthroot - *Trillium erectum*
Bishop's Cap - *Mitella diphylla*
Bittersweet, Asiatic- *Celastrus*
Blackberry, Common - *Rubus allegheniensis*
Black-eyed Susan - *Rudbeckia serotina*
Bleeding Heart - *Dicentra spectabilis*

Bloodroot - *Sanguinaria canadensis*
Blue Curls - *Trichostema dichotomum*
Bluebead - *Clintonia borealis*
Bluebells, Virginia - *Mertensia virginica*
Blueberry, Early Low - *Vaccinium angustifolium*
Blueberry, Highbush - *Vaccinium corymbosum*
Blueberry, Swamp - *Vaccinium corymbosum*
Blue-eyed Grass - *Sisyrinchium*
Bluets - *Houstonia caerulea*
Boneset - *Eupatorium perfoliatum*
Bouncing Bet - *Saponaria officinalis*
Bugle - *Ajuga reptans*
Bugleweed, Northern - *Lycopus unifloris*
Bugleweed, Virginia - *Lycopus virginicus*
Bunchberry - *Cornus canadensis*
Burdock, Common - *Arctium minus*
Bur Marigold, Larger - *Bidens laevis*
Bur Marigold, Nodding - *Bidens cernua*
Butter-and-eggs - *Linaria vulgaris*
Buttercup - *Ranunculus*
Buttonbush - *Cephalanthus occidentalis*
Camphorweed - *Heterotheca subaxillaris*
Campion, Bladder - *Silene cucubalus*
Campion, White - *Lychnis alba*
Cancerroot, One-flowered - *Orobanche uniflora*
Carrot, Wild - *Daucus carota*
Catfoot- *Gnaphalium obtusifolium*
Cat's Ear - *Hypochoeris radicata*
Cattail - *Typha*
Cattail, Common - *Typha latifolia*
Cattail, Narrow-leaved - *Typha angustifolia*
Celandine - *Chelidonium majus*
Centaury - *Centaurium umbellatum*
Checkerberry - *Gaultheria procumbens*

Cherry, Bird - *Prunus pensylvanica*
Cherry, Fire - *Prunus pensylvanica*
Cherry, Pin - *Prunus pensylvanica*
Chickweed, Field - *Cerastium arvense*
Chicory - *Cichorium intybus*
Chokeberry - *Pyrus*
Chokeberry, Black - *Pyrus melanocarpa*
Chokecherry - *Prunus virginiena*
Cinquefoil, Common - *Potentilla simplex*
Cinquefoil, Dwarf - *Potentilla canadensis*
Cinquefoil, Rough - *Potentilla norvegica*
Cinquefoil, Rough-fruited - *Potentilla recta*
Cinquefoil, Silvery - *Potentilla argentea*
Cinquefoil, Sulphur - *Potentilla recta*
Clintonia, Yellow - *Clintonia borealis*
Clover, White Sweet - *Melilotus alba*
Cohosh, Black - *Cimicifuga racemosa*
Cohosh, Blue - *Caulophyllum thalictroides*
Coltsfoot - *Tussilago farfara*
Columbine, European - *Aquilegia vulgaris*
Columbine, Garden - *Aquilegia vulgaris*
Columbine, Wild - *Aquilegia canadensis*
Comfrey, Common - *Symphytum officinale*
Coneflower, Gray-headed - *Ratibida pinnata*
Coneflower, Green-headed - *Rudbeckia laciniata*
Coneflower, Purple - *Echinacea purpurea*
Coneflower, Tall - *Rudbeckia laciniata*
Cornel, Dwarf - *Cornus canadensis*
Corpse Plant - *Monotropa uniflora*
Cowslip - *Caltha palustris*
Cowslip, Virginia - *Mertensia virginica*
Cowwheat - *Melampyrum lineare*
Crab Apple -*Malus*
Cranberry, Highbush - *Viburnum trilobum*

Cranesbill, Spotted - *Geranium maculatum*
Crinkleroot - *Dentaria diphylla*
Crowfoot, Cursed - *Ranunculus sceleratus*
Crowfoot, Small-flowered - *Ranunculus abortivus*
Cuckooflower - *Cardamine pratenses*
Cuckooflower - *Lychnis flos-cuculi*
Cucumber Root, Indian - *Medeola virginiana*
Cucumber, Wild - *Echinocystis lobata*
Cup Plant - *Silphium perfoliatum*
Currant, Garden - *Ribes sativum*
Daffodil - *Narcissus*
Daisy, Oxeye - *Chrysanthemum leucanthemum*
Dandelions - *Taraxacum*
Daphne, February - *Daphne mezereon*
Devil's Paintbrush - *Hieracium aurantiacum*
Dewberry - *Rubus flagellaris*
Dewberry, Swamp - *Rubus hispidus*
Dockmackie - *Viburnum acerifolium*
Dogbane, Spreading - *Apocynun androsa emifolium*
Dogwood, Gray - *Cornus racemosa*
Dogwood, Pale - *Cornus obliqua*
Dogwood, Panicled - *Cornus racemosa*
Dogwood, Red-osier - *Cornus Solonifera*
Dogwood, Round-leaved - *Cornus rugosa*
Dogwood, Silky - *Cornus amomum*
Doll's Eyes - *Actaea pachypoda*
Dutchman's Breeches - *Dicentra*
Elder, Common - *Sambucus canadensis*
Elder, Red-berried - *Sambucus pubens*
Evening Primrose, Common - *Oenothera biennis*
Everlasting, Pearly - *Anaphalis margaritacea*
Everlasting, Sweet - *Gnaphalium obtusifolium*
Feverfew - *Chrysanthemum parthenium*
Fleabane, Common - *Erigeron philadelphicus*

Fleabane, Daisy - *Erigeron annuus*
Fleabane, Lesser Daisy - *Erigeron strigosus*
Fleabane, Philadelphia - *Erigeron philadelphicus*
Foamflower - *Tiarella cordifolia*
Forget-me-not, Smaller - *Myosotis laxa*
Forsythia - *Forsythia*
Gall-of-the-earth - *Prenanthes trifoliata*
Gentian, Bottle - *Gentiana clausa*
Gentian, Closed - *Gentiana clausa*
Geranium, Wild - *Geranium maculatum*
Ghost Pipe - *Orobanche uniflora*
Gill-over-the-ground - *Glechoma hederacea*
Ginger, Wild - *Asarum canadense*
Ginseng, Dwarf - *Panax trifolius*
Goatsbeard, Yellow - *Tragopogon pratensis*
Goldenrod - *Solidago*
Goldenrod, Blue-stemmed - *Solidago caesia*
Goldenrod, Broad-leaved - *Solidago flexicaulis*
Goldenrod, Wreath - *Solidago caesia*
Goldenrod, Zigzag - *Solidago flexicaulis*
Goldenthread - *Coptis groenlandica*
Hardhack - *Spiraea tomentosa*
Hawkweed, Field - *Hieracium pratense*
Hawkweed, Orange - *Hieracium aurantiacum*
Hawkweed, Panicled - *Hieracium paniculatum*
Hawthorn - *Crataegus*
Heal-all - *Prunella vulgaris*
Heliotrope, Garden - *Valeriana officinalis*
Hellebore, False - *Veratrum viride*
Hellebore, White - *Veratrum viride*
Helleborine - *Epipactis helleborine*
Hemp, Indian - *Apocynum cannabinum*
Hepatica, Sharp-lobed - *Hepatica acutiloba*
Herb Robert - *Geranium robertianum*

Hobblebush - *Viburnum alnifolium*
Hog Peanut - *Amphicarpa bracteata*
Hollyhock - *Alcea rosea*
Honeysuckle, Bush - *Diervilla lonicera*
Honeysuckle, Hybrid of Morrow's and Tartarian - *Lonicera bella*
Honeysuckle, Morrow's - *Lonicera morrowi*
Honeysuckle, Tartarian - *Lonicera tatarica*
Horehound, Water - *Lycopus americanus*
Horse Balm - *Collinsonia canadensis*
Huckleberry, Dwarf - *Gaylussacia dumosa*
Hydrangea, Wild - *Hydrangea arborescens*
Indian Cup - *Silphium perfoliatum*
Indian Pipe - *Monotropa uniflora*
Indian Turnip - *Arisaema atrorubens*
Innocence - *Houstonia caerulea*
Iris, Crested - *Iris cristata*
Iris, Dwarf - *Iris verna*
Iris, Larger Blue Flag - *Iris versicolor*
Iris, Siberian - *Iris sibirica*
Iris, Vernal - *Iris verna*
Iris, Yellow - *Iris pseudacorus*
Ivy, Ground - *Glechoma hederacea*
Ivy, Poison - *Rhus radicans*
Jack-in-the-pulpit - *Arisaema*
Jacob's Ladder - *Polemonium van-bruntiae*
Jewelweed - *Impatiens capensis*
Joe-Pye Weed, Spotted - *Eupatorium maculatum*
King Devil - *Hieracium pratense*
Knapweed, Spotted - *Centaurea maculosa*
Knotweed, Pink - *Polygonum pensylvanicum*
Lady's Slipper, Pink - *Cypripedium acaule*
Lady's Slipper, Larger Yellow - *Cypripedium calceolus pubescens*

Lady's Smock - *Cardamine pratenses*
Lady's Thumb - *Polygonum persicaria*
Laurel, Mountain - *Kalmia latifolia*
Leek, Wild - *Allium tricoccum*
Lettuce, Tall White - *Prenanthes altissima*
Lettuce, White - *Prenanthes alba*
Lilac - *Syringa*
Lily, Canada - *Lilium canadense*
Lily, Cow - *Nuphar variegatum*
Lily, Day - *Hemerocallis Fulva*
Lily, Meadow - *Lilium canadense*
Lily, Sweet-scented Water - *Nymphaea odorata*
Lily, Trout - *Erthronium americanum*
Lily, Turk's-cap - *Lilium superbum*
Lily, Wild Yellow - *Lilium canadense*
Lily, Yellow Pond - *Nuphar variegatum*
Lily-of-the-valley - *Convallaria majalis*
Lily-of-the-valley, Wild - *Maianthemum canadense*
Lion's Foot - *Prenanthes trifoliata*
Lobelia, Great - *Lobelia siphilitica*
Lobelia, Spiked - *Lobelia spicata*
Loosestrife, Four-leaved - *Lysimachia quadrifolia*
Loosestrife, Fringed - *Lysimachia ciliata*
Loosestrife, Garden - *Lysimachia vulgaris*
Loosestrife, Purple - *Lythrum salicaria*
Loosestrife, Whorled - *Lysimachia quadrifolia*
Loosestrife, Yellow - *Lysimachia terrestris*
Lousewort - *Pedicularis canadensis*
Lucerne - *Medicago sativa*
Lupine, Garden - *Lupinus polyphyllus*
Maleberry - *Lyonia ligustrina*
Mallow, Musk - *Malva moschata*
Mandarin, Rose - *Streptopus roseus*
Mandrake - *Podophyllum peltatum*

Marigold, Marsh - *Caltha palustris*
Mayapple - *Podophyllum peltatum*
Mayflower - *Epigaea repens*
Mayflower, Canada - *Maianthemum canadense*
Meadow Rue, Early - *Thalictrum dioicum*
Meadow Rue, Tall - *Thalictrum Polygamum*
Meadowsweet - *Spiraea latifolia*
Meadowsweet, Narrow-leaved - *Spiraea alba*
Milfoil - *Achillea millefolium*
Milkweed, Common - *Asclepias syriaca*
Milkweed, Swamp - *Asclepias incarnata*
Mint, Wild - *Mentha arvensis*
Miterwort - *Mitella diphylla*
Miterwort, False - *Tiarella cordifolia*
Moccasin Flower - *Cypripedium acaule*
Moneywort - *Lysimachia nummularia*
Monkshood, Wild - *Aconitum uncinatum*
Motherwort - *Leonurus cardiaca*
Mountain Mint, Narrow-leaved - *Pycnanthemum tenuifolium*
Mouse Ear - *Hieracium pilosella*
Mullein, Common - *Verbascum thapsus*
Mustard, Garlic - *Alliaria officinalis*
Mustard, Hedge - *Sisymbrium officinale*
Myrtle - *Vinca minor*
Nannyberry - *Viburnum lentago*
Nettle, Tall - *Urtica procera*
Nettle, Wood - *Laportea canadensis*
Nightshade, Bittersweet - *Solanum dulcamara*
Nightshade, Enchanter's - *Circaea quadrisulcata*
Nipplewort - *Lapsana communis*
Oswego Tea - *Monarda didyma*
Pansy, Field - *Viola Kitaibeliana*
Parsnip, Wild - *Pastinaca sativa*

Peppermint - *Mentha piperita*
Phlox, Wild Blue - *Phlox divaricata*
Pinesap - *Monotropa hypopithys*
Pink, Maiden - *Dianthus deltoides*
Pinkweed - *Polygonum pensylvanicum*
Pinxter Flower - *Rhododendron nudiflorum*
Plantain, Robin's - *Erigeron pulchellus*
Poke, Indian - *Veratrum viride*
Pokeweed - *Phytolacca americana*
Primrose, Bird's-eye - *Primula laurentiana*
Primrose, Polyanthus - *Primula polyantha*
Privet - *Ligustrum vulgare*
Pussytoes, Canada - *Antennaria canadensis*
Pussytoes, Field - *Antennaria neglecta*
Quaker Ladies - *Houstonia caerulea*
Queen Anne's Lace - *Daucus carota*
Quince, Flowering - *Chaenomeles speciosa*
Radish, Wild - *Raphanus raphanistrum*
Ragged Robin - *Lychnis flos-cuculi*
Ragwort, Golden - *Senecio aureus*
Ragwort, Round-leaved - *Senecio obovatus*
Ramps - *Allium tricoccum*
Raspberry, Black - *Rubus occidentalis*
Raspberry, Purple-flowering - *Rubus odoratus*
Rattlesnake Root - *Prenanthes*
Rattlesnake Root, Boott's - *Prenanthes boottii*
Rattlesnake Root, Tall - *Prenanthes trifoliata*
Rattlesnake Weed - *Hieracium venosum*
Rhododendron - *Rhododendron*
Richweed - *Collinsonia canadensis*
Rocket, Dame's - *Hesperis matronalis*
Rocket, Yellow - *Barbarea vulgaris*
Rose, Multiflora - *Rosa multiflora*
Rose, Rugosa - *Rosa rugosa*

Rose, Smooth - *Rosa blanda*
Rosybells - *Streptopus roseus*
Sandwort, Blunt-leaved - *Arenaria lateriflora*
Sandwort, Grove - *Arenaria lateriflora*
Sarsaparilla, Wild - *Aralia nudicaulis*
Scabious, Sweet - *Erigeron annuus*
Scilla, Siberian - *Scilla sibirica*
Selfheal - *Prunella vulgaris*
Shadbush, Common - *Amelanchier arborea*
Shadbush, Smooth - *Amelanchier laevis*
Shepherd's Purse - *Capsella bursa-pastoris*
Shinleaf - *Pyrola elliptica*
Shooting Star - *Dodecatheon meadia*
Silverrod - *Solidago bicolor*
Skullcap, Mad-dog - *Scutellaria lateriflora*
Skullcap, Marsh - *Scutellaria epilobifolia*
Skunk Cabbage - *Symplocarpus foetidus*
Smartweed, Common - *Polygonum hydropiper*
Smartweed, Dock-leaved - *Polygonum lapathifolium*
Smartweed, Nodding - *Polygonum lapathifolium*
Smartweed, Pale - *Polygonum lapathifolium*
Smartweed, Swamp - *Polygonum coccineum*
Snakeroot, Black - *Cimicifuga racemosa*
Snakeroot, Smaller White - *Eupatorium aromaticum*
Snakeroot, White - *Eupatorium rugosum*
Snowdrop - *Galanthus nivalis*
Snowdrop, Early - *Galanthus nivalis*
Soapwort - *Saponaria officinalis*
Solomon's Seal, False - *Smilacina racemosa*
Solomon's Seal, Great - *Polygonatum canaliculatum*
Solomon's Seal, Hairy - *Polygonatum pubescens*
Sorrel, Common Wood - *Oxalis montana*
Sorrel, Yellow Wood - *Oxalis europaea*
Spatterdock - *Nuphar variegatum*

Speedwell, Bird's-eye - *Veronica chamaedrys*
Speedwell, Common - *Veronica officinalis*
Speedwell, Germander - *Veronica chamaedrys*
Spikenard, Wild - *Smilacina racemosa*
Spiraea - *Spiraea*
Spring Beauty, Carolina - *Claytonia caroliniana*
Spurge, Japanese - *Pachysandra terminalis*
Squill, Spring - *Scilla sibirica*
St. Johnswort, Common - *Hypericum perforatum*
St. Johnswort, Marsh - *Hypericum virginicum*
St. Johnswort, Spotted - *Hypericum punctatum*
Starflower - *Trientalis Boealis*
Steeplebush - *Spiraea tomentosa*
Sticktight - *Bidens frondosa*
Stitchwort, Lesser - *Stellaria graminea*
Stoneroot - *Collinsonia canadensis*
Strawberry - *Fragaria*
Strawberry, Wild - *Fragaria Virginiana*
Strawberry, Wood - *Fragaria vesca*
Sundrops - *Oenothera fruticosa*
Sundrops, Small - *Oenothera perennis*
Sunflower, Pale-leaved - *Helianthus strumosus*
Sunflower, Showy - *Helianthus laetiflorus*
Sunflower, Thin-leaved - *Helianthus decapetalus*
Swamp Candles - *Lysimachia terrestris*
Tansy - *Tanacetum vulgare*
Tearthumb, Arrow-leaved - *Polygonum sagittatum*
Thimbleberry - *Rubus occidentalis*
Thimbleweed - *Anemone virginiana*
Thistle, Bull - *Cirsium vulgare*
Thistle, Canada - *Cirsium arvense*
Thoroughwort - *Eupatorium perfoliatum*
Tick Trefoil, Pointed-leaved - *Desmodium glutinosum*
Toadshade - *Trillium sessile*

Toothwort - *Dentaria diphylla*
Touch-me-not, Spotted - *Impatiens capensis*
Trefoil, Birdsfoot - *Lotus corniculatus*
Trillium, Large-flowered - *Trillium grandiflorum*
Trillium, Nodding - *Trillium cernuum*
Trillium, Painted - *Trillium undulatum*
Trillium, Purple - *Trillium erectum*
Trillium, Red - *Trillium erectum*
Trillium, Toad - *Trillium sessile*
Turtlehead - *Chelone glabra*
Turtlehead, Pink - *Chelone lyoni*
Twisted Stalk, Rose - *Streptopus reseus*
Valerian, Garden - *Vareriana officinalis*
Varerian, Greek - *Polemonium reptans*
Vervain, Blue - *Verbena hastata*
Vervain, White - *Verbena urticifolia*
Vetch, Cow - *Vicia cracca*
Vetch, Tufted - *Vicia cracca*
Viburnum, Maple-leaved - *Viburnum acerifolium*
Vibernum, Sweet - *Viburnum lentago*
Violet - *Viola*
Violet, Dame's - *Hesperis matronalis*
Virgin's Bower - *Clematis virginiana*
Wake-robin - *Trillium erectum*
Water Pepper - *Polygonum hydropiper*
Watercress - *Nasturtium officinale*
Waterleaf, Virginia - *Hydrophyllum virginianum*
Wild Oats - *Uvularia sessilifolia*
Willow Herb, Hairy - *Epilobium hirsutum*
Willow Herb, Northern - *Epilobium glandulosum*
Willow Herb, Purple-leaved - *Epilobium coloratum*
Windflower - *Anemone quinquefolia*
Winter Cress, Common - *Barbarea vulgaris*
Wintergreen - *Gaultheria procumbens*

Woodruff - *Asperula odorata*
Yarrow - *Achillea millefolium*

INDEX

A

M

R

S